# Sixteen Days
## in the Bob Marshall Wilderness

by

David J. Stoltzfus

# Foreword

I never thought while growing up in the plain community of southeastern Pennsylvania and becoming a member in the Amish church that I would ever write a book about hiking. I always loved to travel and see places, but hiking for weeks at a time, and writing about it, was not on my to-do list until I was in my upper twenties.

In my teenage years I was no stranger to camping though. The summer I was eighteen, three of us went on a weeklong canoeing trip on the beautiful Juniata River. We floated about eighty miles in five days. There was no concern about weight, and we had easy access to food along the way. We kept the food in the canoes in sealed, five gallon buckets.

The following year four of us went on a weeklong trip with horses on the Horseshoe Trail. The trail runs through Chester, Berks, Lancaster, Lebanon, and Dauphin counties, and ties into the famous Appalachian Trail in Dauphin County, PA.

The first year was in 2000. We started at Valley Forge Park where George Washington and his troops were camped during the Revolutionary War. We rode through the Park to the trailhead, and in five days we rode about seventy miles to Lancaster County.

The following year we rode the rest of the trail from Lancaster to the Appalachian Trail in Dauphin County. The total distance of the Horseshoe trail is about 140 miles, plus three miles on the Appalachian Trail to the road where our trucker picked us up.

Riding horseback was a great experience. It took a lot of planning to figure out where to get feed for the horses, finding a packsaddle and a mule to carry it, plus we always had to take care of our horses. But this is a story for another book. This chapter is a short story of the events in my life that led to the sixteen day Bob Marshall Wilderness hike.

When I turned twenty-one I wanted to milk cows. Actually, I knew I wanted to milk cows long before I was twenty-one. For thirteen years I was a dairy farmer.

In my mid-twenties I started deer hunting and was hooked.

In the year of 2008 five of us went on a road trip to the west for three weeks. We toured Yellowstone, WY; Glacier Park, MT; The Badlands, SD; and other short stops in between.

We camped a lot on that trip and never slept in a hotel. Twice we slept in a cabin at a campground, but we mostly slept in our tents or under the stars.

At Glacier Park, MT, we had intended to do a three-day backpacking tour. But that year, in early June when we were there, the snow up in the passes was too deep to hike across. Even the Going-to-the-Sun Road was still closed. So we just camped at a campground for a couple days and did a few day hikes. That early in the season the wildlife hadn't moved to higher ground and we saw much wildlife.

We also did a week of volunteer work at a ranch close to East Glacier where a wildfire had done a lot of damage. The rancher's name was Doc Hammell. He was a horse trainer and taught people how to work with large draft horses. That week we rebuilt fence that was burnt, fixed a burnt manure spreader, and a few other small things.

On June 10 we had a snowstorm that snowed ten inches while back east there was sweltering heat. We holed up in the cabin during the storm.

This ranch was located right against the Lewis and Clark National forest that borders the Bob Marshall Wilderness on the north side. Doc Hammell told us that south of him there stretched an unbroken wilderness with no roads or houses for a hundred miles. I was intrigued. I decided if I ever get the chance I would be back to either hunt elk or hike this great country. But I knew that to do this I would need to quit milking cows.

For seven years I kept on milking cows.

In the summer of 2012 four of us went on a canoeing and hiking trip in the Adirondack Mountains of New York. We were gone for eight days. We left on a Saturday, did a three-day canoe route until Tuesday afternoon, then hiked the high peaks another three days. It was a great experience, canoeing, fishing, and hiking in the Adirondacks, but my ultimate dream was to do another trip to the remote areas in the West.

I had hired one of the neighbor men to help with the cows, but I knew that to take three or four weeks off, the cows would have to go. My father was now in his lower seventies, and the responsibility of managing the farm while I went on trips was becoming too much.

In the spring of 2015 things reached a climax. The milk price had crashed that winter, my father had a few health issues, good weekend help was hard to find, and I didn't see any sense in a single man like me to keep on milking cows.

It was a heartrending decision. For over seventy years the barn had held cows that needed to be milked twice every day. For the last thirteen years they were a part of me and in a way they were like part of the family. But I also knew that I don't have to milk cows, the circumstances were what they were, and everything seemed to be pointing in the direction to quit.

In February I made the decision to sell my cows by April or May. Around that time I heard that Elam Beiler was planning a trip to the Bob Marshall Wilderness. In 2012 he had taken a trip in the Bob with some other friends, and as I pondered the possibility of going along, I decided that now is my chance. In March I put my name in to go along.

In the first week of May my cows left for the sale barn. It wasn't easy to see them go, but I never doubted that I had done the right thing. Now it was time to move into the next phase in life. Sometimes God asks us to quit doing what we love to do so we can do what he wants us to do. Knowing what he wants us to do can be hard and it can feel like we are at a dead end. But, as long as we have breath and life in our bodies there are no dead ends.

It can be a lot like hiking on a wilderness trail. The trail may take a sharp bend ahead of us where we cannot see around it, but we believe a glorious scene awaits us. Rarely can we see for long distances ahead of us and see what awaits us at the end.

Life is also a lot like climbing a mountain. It can be a long, tough climb and many times we pause to rest, but we know if we keep going it will be worth the effort once we reach the top. The views are awesome at the top, but we also know we cannot stay up there forever.

At the top we usually have three choices. If the trail goes on we can cross over, down into the next valley. If the trail ends at the top we can make our own trail down to the next valley, or, we can turn around and go down the way we came up and circle around into the next valley.

A lot like the choices we have to make in this life. One choice may not be more right or wrong than the other one, but may lead us in a different direction for a while. But if we follow God's will, which is to have faith and to love one another, we will all meet at the same place where there is only love, peace, and joy. For some it may take longer than others, but if we have faith and trust in God, we will eventually reach our goal.

Once my cows were sold I had only two months to train and prepare for the trip to the wilderness. The first thing I did was order a new backpack. I needed one large enough to hold sixteen days worth of food and gear. I used my brother's pack on my other trips, but that pack weighed twelve pounds empty. Elam had bought a pack that held 6,000 cubic inches, weighed only seven pounds, and had all kinds of adjustments. It was built by Tenzing and was by far the best hiking-hunting pack I had ever seen. The price was almost four hundred dollars, but I knew if I wanted to do this a good pack is a must, and besides, if I went on hunting trips I would need a good pack, too. I bought one, and I never regretted it.

Once I had the pack, the first thing I did was fill it up with thirty pounds of books. The first week I walked a couple miles three or four times. Thirty pounds became heavy after a couple miles and I wondered how I'm going to make it, for my goal was to reach sixty pounds by the second week of July. But I knew from experience that to do a hike like that a person needs to prepare himself mentally as well as physically. By the end of the first week the thirty pounds carried much better. The following week I added ten more pounds. This I kept doing every week until a couple of weeks before the trip I was up to sixty-four pounds. I also did some running to build lung capacity.

With all the training I was doing I felt more physically fit than I had since I was a teenager. It took a lot of effort and time, but I knew if I wanted to do this I would never regret the time I spent in training once we were in the wilderness.

The next step was planning the food and gear to take along. This was perhaps the most challenging part of the planning process. Weight was a big deal. One rule of thumb is for every pound you can cut in weight, you pay an extra hundred dollars.

One example is rain gear. You can go to the Wal-Mart and buy rainpants and a jacket for maybe twenty or thirty dollars that will keep you dry. But it might weigh two or three pounds while Cabela's has raingear that costs 150 dollars and weighs a pound or less.

These were some of the decisions I had to make. I knew from previous hikes that every pound you can eliminate is a big deal. Once you have your pack strapped to your back and are on the trail in the wilderness for two weeks you quickly realize that inferior gear, just to save a few dollars, is not worth it.

I had a lightweight tent and sleeping bag from previous trips so I knew I'm good there. Since it was a summertime trip I would pack light in clothes. A fleece sweater, one pair of pants, a shirt, several changes of underwear, a tee shirt, swimming trunks, seven pairs of socks, a warm cap for cold mornings, and a floppy hat with a wide brim to shield my head from the bright sun made up the pile of clothes for sixteen days. I bought a rainsuit from Cabela's, the good kind that is lightweight.

Fishing gear was a must, for we intended to fish for food. This was a fishing trip as much as a hiking trip. I borrowed a lightweight fly rod from a friend who had been in the Bob with Elam in 2012. The fly rod came apart in short lengths and packed very nicely with my collapsible spinning rod in the side pocket of my new backpack. The spinning rod I had bought before we took our New York trip in the Adirondacks. I also took binoculars, a pocket testament, a writing tablet, my Leatherman pocket knife, a sleeping pad, and a few other small things.

For drinking water I took a hand pump with a filter on it to pump right out of the streams into my three-liter water bladder that had its own pocket in my pack. I had some water purifying tablets just in case my filter quit working.

For eating and cooking utensils, I took a small cookstove and a couple one-pound cans of butane gas, an eighteen ounce cup to boil water in and to drink out of, plus two plastic sporks. A first aid kit, and what I thought was plenty of duct tape, a headlamp, a small towel, bear and mosquito spray, finished my stash. Now my pack weighed thirty-two pounds and I still had thirty pounds of food to pack.

Packing food was one of the biggest challenges of the packing process. For the average hike in mountainous areas, three thousand calories a day is about the daily minimum. That was the rule of the thumb that I went by, which averaged about one hundred calories per ounce of food. The easiest way to reach the hundred calories per ounce is with chocolate candy. Some chocolates are as high as two hundred ten calories per ounce or more. But eating only chocolate is not a very balanced diet, and we had to look at the nutrition side, too. Dove chocolate candy is one of my favorites. It comes in small wrapped pieces in different flavors, packs at least two hundred calories an ounce, packs well, and makes a very tasty snack with a shot of energy. I allowed myself four pieces each day.

Nuts are next in calories per ounce. Pecans, almonds, pistachios, pine nuts, and sunflower seeds all range from one hundred sixty to two hundred calories per ounce and make very tasty snacks. I always preferred individually packed nuts over trail mix. Just a personal preference.

Peanut butter, olive oil, coconut oil, and butter all range around two hundred calories an ounce. I took a one pound jar of peanut butter, and when we heard that we can't have fire west of the Continental Divide, we bought two eight-ounce bottles of olive oil and a small pan to cook fish on our butane campstoves.

Granola bars and granola cereal finished the heavier food. For the lightweight foods I took three or four mountain house meals, ramen noodles, packets of maple-flavored oatmeal, packs of Lance crackers, Swiss Miss chocolate packets, and for a sweetener I added two eight-ounce jars of honey.

I also added several packs of dried fruit. Dried mangoes are my favorite, but I added some dried pineapple for more variety. Dried fruit isn't as high in calories, only about eighty calories per ounce, but the added flavor to a meal or snack is well worth it, plus more nutrition.

I brought dried milk to mix with my granola cereal. I couldn't find any whole dried milk so I settled with low-fat, dried milk. Dried milk is better than nothing, but there were times on our trip that I longed for a tall glass of fresh, ice cold milk. There were certain things in the wilderness that we could not have. But then there were things we never have at home, like fresh mountain trout, wild huckleberries, raspberries, and ice cold water out of a mountain stream. Then there were the views, but we'll get to that later. The small salt shaker with salt for fish we intended to catch for food finished my food supply. I figured I could survive in the wilderness for sixteen days among the wild animals.

For a little extra nutrition I sweet-talked my nieces into packing a mixture of protein shakes and vitamins in small packets. A company by the name of Reliv makes some very good nutritional products and protein shakes that do a great job in balancing trail food and keeps the digestive system in order. Everything is in powder form, is lightweight, packs easily, and needs only to be mixed with water to take it. They pack a lot of energy; by taking one pack a day, it doesn't take as much food and helps maintain body weight. I added half a dozen packs of powdered Gatorade to add to my drinking water on warm days. The electrolytes in the Gatorade helped keep energy levels up on hot days, and I wished I would have taken enough for the whole trip, for it added flavor.

Packing everything was a challenge. At the Wal-Mart I had bought small and large Ziploc plastic bags, the kind that have a sliding closure. One bag for underwear, one for socks, some empty ones for dirty clothes, and the food that wasn't in sealed packs I packed in the Ziplocs.

I didn't go exactly at the three thousand calories a day rule but used it as a guide. The one hundred calories per ounce rule helped in making decisions on what to buy.

By the beginning of July I had most of my food bought, my training had gone well, with my pack weight up to sixty four pounds. On July, 14 2015, our train was scheduled to leave at 2:40 P.M. What we had been planning for months was suddenly almost here.

The night before we left I invited my nieces over to a packing party. Many willing hands made it a pleasant experience as we counted out the chocolates, oatmeal, Swiss miss, noodles in several different flavors, nuts, mountain house meals, cereal, until we had enough for sixteen days. Then we packed it in Ziploc bags and stuffed it in my backpack. Everything went in that I wanted to, although, the way we crammed some of it in I knew it wouldn't be in the same shape when I took it out as it was when we packed it. But that didn't matter, because on hiking trips a person doesn't concern himself how his food looks as long as it is in edible condition.

The morning of July 14, I finished packing everything. My backpack weighed over sixty pounds and the suitcase I had packed with clothes to wear in Rexford and on the train weighed around forty pounds. Finally, after weeks of preparation, training, planning, packing and sweating, the day of departure had arrived.

# Chapter One: The Journey

1.

We are headed for the west,
Where the scenery is best.
Where the mountain lions roam,
In the grizzly bears' home.
Where the coyotes growl,
And the great wolves howl.

2.

The trout in the streams,
Taste like our sweetest dreams.
The mountains are high,
In the land of the big sky.
The waters are clear,
With no houses near.

3.

The trees are pine,
With scents so fine.
The views are vast,
The memories last.
The fourteenth of July,
Is when we say goodbye.

4.

To go on vacation,
At the train station.
When you think of me,
Wherever that may be.
Just say a little prayer,
For us way out there.

On July 14, 2015, we headed for Rexford, Montana, via Amtrak. There was three of us: Elam Beiler, Mervin Smucker, and myself. We started from Lancaster at 2:00 P.M. and arrived in Pittsburgh at 7:30 P.M.

The trip to Pittsburgh was uneventful and the train to leave Pittsburgh was an hour late, so we did some sightseeing.

We walked to a place that is called The Point, about a mile from the train station. It is the place where the Allegheny and the Monongahela Rivers meet to form the great Ohio River. There used to be a fort right at The Point with blockhouses at the corners. On the grass it was marked where the old fort stood. There is a stone building that was used for a fort and was built later. It is now a museum but it was closed when we were there.

We were hungry as we headed for the Market Square for something to eat. On the way we went under a bridge with an arch that had a wide walkway underneath it with water under and on each side of the walkway. There was a group of young people on the walkway singing songs. They had guitars and speakers to amplify the sound. The architecture of the bridge and the water with the lighting made it sound nice, and we talked about bringing out our youth group to Pittsburgh to sing under that bridge. There would be room for at least a hundred people on the walkway. It would be neat, but I have strong doubts that it will ever happen. Singing in the wilderness would be better than in the city anyhow.

From there we went to the Market Square where we filled ourselves with pizza. It was late when we got back to the station, but we still had to wait for two hours.

We had met Mose Esh and his wife at Lancaster. It was nice to travel with someone we knew so well and could visit with them at Pittsburgh. They were headed to Elkhart, Indiana, for a wedding. Now there wasn't much to do except wait for our train.

We finally left Pittsburgh at 1:15 A.M. on July 15. We were due in Chicago at 8:45 A.M. but didn't arrive until 12:30 P.M., almost four hours late. There were a lot of freight trains holding up our train.

While travelling through Ohio, an Amish couple boarded the train. I met the man at the lounge car where we talked for about an hour. They were travelling to Texas with their two teenage children, a boy and girl, to visit friends.

We had an interesting talk. When he heard that we planned to stay in Rexford Montana for the weekend, he said that a niece of his lived there and was dating a fellow whose name was Ben Fisher. Ben was originally from Pennsylvania, although I didn't know him.

The man's name was Ammon Yoder, and in the course of our conversation he asked me to say hello to his niece Cindy Miller for him when I saw her. I said I would if I get the chance.

This seemed like a tall order for me, for I had no idea what she looked like and besides, I didn't know a soul in Rexford. "Oh well," I thought, "I'll just have to see what happens and if I figure out who she is I'll do it one way or the other." I still had several days until I would see her. Besides, she might be at her boyfriend's place in Lewistown for the weekend. At any rate I didn't intend to worry much about it.

At the station in Chicago we carried our heavy luggage into the huge station and wondered what to do with it while we find something to eat. We each had around a hundred pounds of luggage in our backpacks and suitcases and we were hungry. The Empire Builder was due to leave at 2:15 P.M.

We met a young Amish fellow from Illinois who was sitting in the waiting room with his luggage. His train wasn't leaving until 4:00. We asked him if he would watch our luggage while we grabbed a bite to eat. He gladly watched our luggage. We left our luggage in his care and went out on the street to see what we could find.

We found a Subway shop and each of us ordered a foot-long sub with a drink. We went to a small park and sat on the grass to eat. It was a nice day, and the food was good.

There were people everywhere: on the sidewalks, in the cars in the streets, and in the park. I was glad we are not staying there long, and I looked forward to wilderness solitude. I would rather see high mountains and wildlife than these tall buildings and all the people. Every time I go to a city and see all the people, I wonder where everybody is going and what they will do when they

3

get there. Some people look happy, some look sad, and a lot don't have much expression. Some are homeless and live on the streets begging. Each person lives their own life and no one is the same, but we were all created by the same God who created us for his pleasure. Mind-boggling.

But I am getting off my story. We finished our meal and headed back to the station to our luggage. The young fellow was still watching our luggage and it looked like he hadn't had any problem with it. But he had a different story.

Soon after we left the station the station police came and asked him if he knows these guys with this luggage. He couldn't say that he did. Apparently it looked suspicious to the police when we walked in there with our heavy backpacks and suitcases and talked a little with this guy, dropped our luggage, and left. They suspected us enough that they brought in dogs to sniff our luggage for anything that we weren't supposed to have. Of course the dogs didn't find anything so they left our luggage alone. We were thankful that they didn't open anything and scatter our stuff around. They were just doing their job.

We thanked the young fellow, and by then it was time to board our train to leave for Montana. We never got the young man's name, one thing I often regret. It was a reminder of the privilege we have to trust complete strangers if they are dressed plainly and speak our language. Another thing I've often taken for granted and don't often think about it.

We left Chicago, Wednesday at 2:15 P.M. on the Empire Builder, due in Whitefish, Montana, on Thursday evening.

We met some colorful characters on the train. One man we met in the lounge car was an engineer in technology. He was from Missouri, and he programmed computers for medical units.

He asked us about our lifestyle and wondered about the Amish Mafia. We tried to explain to him that we choose this lifestyle because we wanted it, not because we had to. We assured him that we never even heard about the Amish Mafia before the Discovery Channel aired it on television. It's amazing how many outside people wonder if it is true. Here we are supposed to be a non-resistant group and a TV show portrays the complete opposite. Most people don't really believe it but they still wonder about it. The Discovery Channel is supposed to be true. I guess to them if they can make a lot of money off of it, it doesn't matter.

Some people, even if they don't believe it find it very entertaining, and for others it turns them off that a TV show exploits a peace-loving religious group. And when we have the opportunity to explain to people (like the man from Missouri) that there is no basis in the show, they seem to be relieved.

We talked for a while with the man from Missouri. He had a lot of questions about our lifestyle and it seemed like he felt that it would be a great way to live. But as is always the case, for someone like him to change to such a lifestyle, it looks like an insurmountable mountain.

Talking with people like that, on trips like this, always makes me appreciate our heritage like never before.

I never got the man's name. He went to another part of the train after a while.

At one of the stations a man came on board and sat beside me in the lounge car. He struck up a conversation and soon made it known that he had to have alcohol. Amtrak serves alcohol, and he soon found out where it is. His name was Ed Simmons. He was born in 1958, had been all over the states, and right now he was headed for Billings, Montana. His birthplace was in Alaska, he looked older than sixty-seven, and I felt sorry for him. He looked like a troubled man. He said he is the son of a preacher. He also said he wears a bracelet on his ankle so his son knows where he is at all times. I didn't know what all to believe, although he was interesting.

Apparently Ed wasn't used to travelling on the train much, because the conductor came into the lounge car and asked where his seat is. Ed didn't have a clue. He came on the train, went through it until he came to the lounge car, and sat on the empty seat beside me. It didn't look like he had much luggage. The conductor took him to another car, and before he left Ed made sure to tell me to reserve his seat beside me. Nobody tried to claim his seat and he was soon back.

Soon he went back to the café car and came back with more beer and whiskey. He complained about the pricey stuff, but he claimed he had to have it. He also was a smoker, and he would go down to the lower level and smoke in the restrooms, something that was prohibited on the train.

Ed had serious problems in his life. A group of four women came in the lounge car and sat at one of the tables not far from us. By that time his tongue was loose from the alcohol and he ranted about women for a while. I sat there listening to him talk, not knowing what to say. He did talk a little about the Amish, how he respects us a lot for our lifestyle and the way we live and believe. But somewhere in his life he must have had some rough experiences, which he allowed himself to become bitter about and he turned to alcohol for solace. I felt sorry for him. Sometimes it's best to just listen when someone goes off like that. It was useless to try and reason with him. Then he quoted a little rhyme that he said he composed. He said : "I remember the days when men were men. If it was up to me I'd bring them back again."

It sounded like he thought men are softies nowadays and don't know how to stand up for themselves. But it was obvious that he had never learned the value of submitting himself to authority, as we shall see what happened to him later on the train.

When Ed heard we were headed for the Bob Marshall Wilderness, he told us a story about a friend of his who had gone to hike in there. This man never came back and nobody ever found a trace of him. It was a scary story, but what he didn't tell us was of the many thousands of people who hike and hunt in the wilderness and always come back. A lot of people like to dwell on the wild animals and the dangers in the wild. I don't know what the percentages are, but I'm sure we ran a lot higher risk of injury on our journey to the wilderness than being in the wilderness itself. One person even suggested we take a baseball bat along to protect ourselves from the bad men that hide from the law in the wilderness.

"Wow," I thought, "I never even thought of that. Maybe we should."

But I figured there would be plenty of clubs around, and if we needed firewood...the club would probably serve the purpose as good as a baseball bat; probably better.

Ed mentioned how he likes our suspenders we were wearing. That made us smile.

Later we met an interesting man whose name was James Wheeler. He was born in 1953, served in the Marines, had been in all fifty states and spent time in Bavaria where he picked up a little German. If a person showed any interest in listening to him he talked on and on.

He also took a strong interest in our way of life. It was humbling to realize how much a lot of people respect and admire our way of life. Another person who helped us see the value of our own heritage.

James built model ships for a hobby, and if he had a listener who showed any interest, he went on and on about how old wooden ships were built and designed. He built model ships in intricate and painstaking detail. He found out that Elam was in construction; that interested him a lot. Elam understood the terminology James was using better than Mervin and I did.

James carried a thick book with him that was about shipbuilding. About in the middle of the book he had a marker where he liked to open and show anybody that listened, a picture of himself building a model boat. Then he explained what he was doing in much detail.

He didn't seem to care much about creature comfort and was dressed a little shabbily. He didn't talk at all about family, and it looked like he was travelling alone. He was headed for Washington State where he wanted to do research on how the Kootenai Indians built their canoes.

Around 10:00 P.M. Central time we arrived in St. Paul, Minnesota, where we were allowed to come off the train for a short break to stretch our legs and the smokers could have a smoke.

After the break I went back to the lounge and sat at a table. I wasn't quite ready to settle down for the night yet in the coach car. A couple of tables away was a dark complexioned, heavyset, muscular man eating a Subway sandwich. He beckoned me to him and asked me to try one of his granola bars. I was hesitant at first, because I didn't know what his motives were.

The granola bar was good. We talked awhile and he told me he is Native American on his father's side and his mother was French Canadian. He was headed for the Kootenai Indian reservation in Northwest Montana where his tribe lived. He planned to hunt elk there. Native Americans may hunt on their reservation whenever they please without a license. And they don't need to pay taxes.

We talked for several hours about both of our ways of living, what we eat, how the Amish are planters and harvesters while his people are hunters and gatherers. He was another person who took a strong interest in our way of living. He had noticed us in Chicago when we went to the Subway shop to buy sandwiches. He followed us into the store and bought his own sandwich. It seemed like he was waiting for the chance to talk with one of us.

His name was Miles. He was a heavyweight lifter and competed in CrossFit competitions. He was a wide muscular man, weighed 280 pounds, and the weights he lifted were as high as 326 pounds. Sitting across the table from him made me feel puny. But he was a friendly person, and at twenty-seven he was in the prime of life. I shared some of my homemade sandwiches that I had along, which he seemed to enjoy a great deal.

# Chapter One: The Journey

I went back to my seat around midnight and slept the best I could on the coach seat. This was our second night on the train, and I was getting used to sleeping in a sitting position. The neck pillow that I had borrowed from my mother helped a lot to keep my head from flopping around while I slept.

Unfortunately both Ed Simmons and Miles got kicked off the train the next morning for disorderly conduct. Ed was a heavy smoker, and he would go to the lower floor of the cars where the restrooms are and light up in one of the out-of-service stalls. This was very much against Amtrak rules, and there was no way to contain the smell in the tiny restrooms. He did it once too often; the conductors caught him and forced him off at the next station somewhere in eastern Montana.

Again I felt sorry for Ed. Somehow in his life he never learned to submit to authority and would get himself into trouble for it. I guess it's been that way since the beginning of time; if we don't obey a higher authority there are consequences. Adam and Eve didn't obey and were driven out of the Garden of Eden. It's something we all need to learn if we want to have law and order.

Miles got kicked off at the same stop for drunkenness. I had gone to the lower level that morning to use the restrooms. The exits from the train are down there too, and there were two of the conductors at the doorway. I talked with them for a little, and they mentioned that they were kicking these guys off. Miles was on a seat at the top of the stairs. He was laying across two seats in a stupor.

The conductors said they are not here to babysit anybody. The night before they had to guide him to his seat because he couldn't find it.

At the same station Ed got kicked off there were two policemen waiting. They quietly came on board, shook Miles awake, told him to get his belongings and hauled him off. Miles didn't put up any resistance and groggily did as he was told. They would have had their hands full if he would have resisted, for he was very strong. But with alcohol in his blood and the sudden awakening, he was too dazed to resist.

Outside, they asked him for his ID. He put his pack down, dug through it until he found it and showed it to the cops. The train pulled away, and that was the last we saw of him.

Then the conductor made a speech on the intercom that they will not tolerate any kind of behavior that goes against Amtrak rules. I deeply respected and admired Amtrak for enforcing the rules. The privilege we have to travel in a system where men and women work hard to ensure comfort and safety is something to be thankful for. But I wondered why they serve alcohol when it causes so many problems. Maybe they make a lot of money from selling alcohol. Often, the mighty dollar comes first. Like the Amish Mafia; it's not true, but somebody is making a lot of money from it so they air it anyway. Alcohol causes many problems but if someone can make money from selling it, they will sell it.

The next entry in my diary was 7:15 P.M. mountain time. By that time we were travelling through central Montana. It was vast, wide open country. In that area a lot of wheat gets farmed. The fields are so vast it boggled my small mind how huge they are. The harvest was still a few weeks away. A lot of oats and barley gets farmed in that area too. Even the sky looked bigger, and I understood why Montana is called the Big Sky Country.

The train was running two and a half hours late because of a derailment of a freight train the day before. They had to replace three miles of track, and there were over one hundred freight trains waiting for the tracks to be fixed. In the West the tracks are owned by the freight companies, where they have the right of way, which often causes delays for Amtrak. An incredible amount of freight gets moved on these tracks every day. Luckily, the freight trains let Amtrak go on before all the freight trains went that were waiting, but even then we didn't expect to come to Whitefish, Montana, (our destination) until 11:30 P.M.

Just before dusk there were dark clouds on the horizon. Soon the sun shone and a beautiful rainbow appeared. The colors were the same as they are in the East. It was awesome. The country was different, but the rainbows looked the same. No matter where a person goes, there are a lot of things that never change.

Right after the plains were the Glacier Park Mountains. It was dark by that time, so we didn't get to see Glacier Park in the daylight—something we regretted a lot.

A family from Minnesota was seated in front of us. They were headed for West Glacier, where they planned to stay a few days at the park. The man's name was Mike Vetch, and he was a dairy farmer in Little Falls, Minnesota. I guessed he would be in his upper forties and they were travelling with their children for a vacation.

They milk two hundred cows and farm corn, alfalfa, and grass hay. It was neat meeting another farmer among all the city people on the train to talk with about cows and farming in general.

This man had never been on much of a vacation before and this was his first time on a train. We talked for a long time about things farmers talk about: crops, cows, weather, prices, and the never-ending challenges of farming.

No matter where I travel, farmers have their own unique challenges that outsiders cannot comprehend or grasp. And when two complete strangers that are farmers meet, there immediately is a bond between them that is hard to explain. Part of the reason is that no matter what size farm, how many cows we milk, if we raise beef, produce, or cash crops, we all deal with a lot of things we don't have control of. Number one is the weather. There are market fluctuations, labor shortages, equipment breakdowns, crop failures, water shortages, expensive land or rent, and a host of things a farmer deals with daily. This all creates a common bond among farmers that I haven't found in any other business group.

There are many different ways to farm and each way has its own unique challenges. But no matter how a person farms, the privilege to grow up on a farm and experience all the different challenges is a valuable experience.

Later that night I met a young man about my age who was also single. He worked in the mission field where he helped smuggle Bibles into China, Vietnam, Nepal, and other countries.

I had seen him earlier talking with Elam and I remember wondering what for hippie Elam was talking to. He had long hair and a bandana tied around his head to keep his hair out of his face. I didn't know what to think of him right away.

Later, I was at one of the lounge car tables where him and another young man were sitting on the lounge seats by the windows. I overheard them talking about hiking and camping in the mountains so I went over and joined them.

We talked about where we are going and about his Bible smuggling. The other fellow soon left for his coach seat as it was almost midnight. The lounge car was almost empty by that time and I believe we would have talked all night long if Mervin wouldn't have come and interrupted us to say that we are nearing Whitefish where our destination was. It was a reminder to be more careful how I judge others by how they look, for this fellow seemed like a really nice person and a sound Christian. I wished we would have had more time to talk. I didn't even get his name.

# Sixteen Days in the Bob Marshall Wilderness

We came off the train in Whitefish at 12:15 A.M. mountain time. We had to walk about a mile with our heavy packs to the hostel that Elam had booked to sleep in for what was left of the night. The hot shower was awesome, the beds were good, and it was nice to stretch out in a true horizontal position to sleep once again. Finally, after two and one half days of travel, we were off the train in Montana.

The next morning we had a good breakfast at a restaurant that was called Crepes. Later we went shopping for final supplies. We stopped at a flyfishing store where I bought flies for bait, sunglasses, watershoes for crossing streams, tippet, and a few odds and ends. Now it was time to quit spending money on gear and go do the real thing. We stopped at a grocery store where I bought two packs of string cheese and a bag of bagels. Now I was all set with food, too.

Our driver to take us to Rexford was at the hostel by 11:00 A.M. His name was Mike Smith. He lived in Rexford and worked for a log cabin builder.

We crammed our heavy backpacks and suitcases into his suburban and headed for Rexford.

We stopped at the post office in Kalispell to get boxes for our suitcases and pay to have them shipped to Fairfield where Dave lived. Dave was the guy whom we had scheduled to pick us up at the trail's end in two and one half weeks. We planned to ship the suitcases on Monday morning on the way to the trailhead.

Oh yes, I remembered that I needed a stuff sack to put food in at night so we could pull it up on a tree branch away from a bear's reach. There was a Sportsman Shop in the same shopping center as the post office. We ran over there where I got the stuff sack and added a whistle to my gear. The other guys bought a few things and now we were set.

*Our first views of the Rocky Mountain front at sunset.*

# Chapter Two: Rexford

From Kalispell it took us about an hour to get to Rexford. We stopped at a Subway in Eureka for sandwiches on the way.

We arrived in Rexford at 2:30. The scenery on the way was awesome. There were mountains and hills. The trees are almost all pines with large Ponderosas, cedars, and the plentiful lodge pole pines. It is so different having mostly evergreens with no leaves. Seeing all these inflammable trees made me realize the real danger that forest fires are. A lot of the houses were built among the trees with highly combustible logs. Some of the log homes were beautiful, just like the pictures that are in magazines of the West.

It was very dry when we were there. There weren't any open fires allowed, anywhere. Even on the Fourth of July they hadn't allowed any fireworks because of the danger of fires.

Mike Smith drove us around the area and we saw where a lot of the Amish live. It's quite different from other Amish settlements, for there are very few farmers or ranchers. A lot of them work in a large furniture shop where they build rustic furniture from pine logs. There are also log home builders, one of them whom Mike worked for as a salesman.

Behind the cabin where we were staying a family by the name of Yoder had their own sawmill and a small shop where they built log furniture. It was quite different from what we are used to, but I was intrigued and found the area very interesting. Mike said there are eighteen bachelors living in the community at the time. I looked forward to meeting them. We planned to go to church and be at their singing on Sunday.

We stopped in at the shop and found Jerry Yoder, the man who was in charge of the cabin where we were staying. He directed us to the cabin—which was only about half a mile away—where we unloaded our heavy backpacks and suitcases and parted ways with Mike until Monday morning when we had him scheduled to pick us up at 6:00 to head to the Bob Marshall Wilderness.

Before we unpacked our suitcases, we decided to go back and tour the shop where we had just came from. Jerry had said they are closing at 3:00, because a lot of the employees were headed for Mt. Robinson on an overnight riding and camping trip.

One thing I learned at Rexford; these guys know how to have fun. To truly love the area a person must love the great out-of-doors, and to not feel left out you need to like to hunt and fish, too. I didn't hear of any bachelors that lived there who do not hunt or fish, and a lot of the girls and women hunt too. Some of the stories these guys had to tell of their hunting and fishing experiences were very good. They have elk, bear, moose, mule and whitetail deer to hunt right in their backyard. Their backyards can go back for many miles compared to around home. They also have the Koocanusa Lake to fish in, located right beside the community. The area is truly an outdoorsman's paradise.

We toured the shop where they built post and log furniture. Jerry showed us how they fitted the pieces together. A lot of the furniture was mortise and tenon like the chairs, bed frames, and tables. The table and chair tops were glued-together panels that they made onsite. They built some high quality, heavy-duty furniture designed to last for many years and was shipped all over the United States.

At the shop we learned about a store at the end of the driveway that had an all-you-can-eat-buffet Friday evening and Saturday morning. This sounded wonderful to us so we stopped in on the way back to our cabin to make reservations. The girl that greeted us at the restaurant-store was very friendly and she soon had supper reservations for the three of us at 7:00. Her friendly attitude and the relaxed atmosphere of the store and restaurant soon put us at ease. I decided we are going to enjoy Rexford if everyone is so friendly and nice as the few people we had met thus far.

We went back to the cabin, unpacked our suitcases, organized out fishing gear and settled in. Elam had a lot of extra flies along. Mervin and I picked out a bunch that we thought might fool a fish into thinking this is a real meal. I tried to pick out the ones that I thought would look good to a fish but I still didn't have a clue. Someone at the fly shop in Whitefish had said black flies are good. I made sure I had some black ones. We planned to fish for bull trout so I bought some large streamers. At three dollars apiece for the large flies and a dollar for the small ones I soon had at least fifty dollars in flies alone. I felt foolish spending so much money on flies when at home I can catch night crawlers for free. But we were going fly fishing in the Bob Marshall Wilderness. I wasn't going to let a few dollars keep me from getting what I thought might look good to a fish. Besides, they probably didn't have night crawlers in the wilderness.

The cabin we were staying in was one of the nicest cabins I had ever seen. It was spotless; we each had our own room with a bed; there was running water, heat, a cookstove with a refrigerator beside it, cooking utensils and everything three guys could wish for on a weekend. There were two full baths, and at one hundred dollars a night it was cheaper and better than most motels.

We had everything except food, and by 7:00 we needed food. We went to the restaurant where we had made reservations.

We were greeted by the same friendly girl as before. We paid the bill, and at thirty-five dollars for the three of us, I hoped the food would be good. We were not disappointed. The buffet was delicious. We stuffed ourselves with mashed potatoes and gravy, smoked turkey, beans, sauerkraut, and for dessert we had a rich pudding. It was great eating a home-cooked meal again, and I looked forward to breakfast in the morning.

The restaurant-store is owned by an Amish couple that moved there from Indiana. They were just living there since May and already they had a lot of customers at the restaurant. We talked with the owner. I asked him if they came for the opportunity and he said, "No, we wanted away from the humidity."

They got away from the humidity all right, for a sweater would have felt good outside in the cool evening air. But I hadn't thought to bring my sweater along so I did without. That morning the temperature had been forty-eight degrees.

We ate our supper outside under the porch roof. The sun was shining brightly but under the roof in the shade it was cool. The low humidity made a big difference because as soon as we stepped into the shade it felt cool, a phenomenon we experienced quite often on our trip.

We were done eating and were sitting at the tables relaxing when a bachelor, whose name was Daniel Mast, came out on the porch with a plateful of

15

food and sat down at our table. He was a friendly man and asked us where we are from and where we are going. We said we are headed for the Bob Marshall Wilderness on Monday morning.

He talked about his experiences in the Bob. He had done a lot of hunting and horseback riding in the wilderness and had shot elk. He wanted to know which area we planned to hike and the trails we would be on. We visited for about an hour while he entertained us with some good hunting stories.

By the time he left, the sun was setting and it was time for us to buy food from the store for the next few days and head back to the cabin. We wanted to buy some hamburger or steak, but all they had in the line of meat was hotdogs and bacon. Then I remembered how Daniel Mast had told us about the elk he had shot. I asked the store owner if I could use the bike that was parked outside to go ask him if he would have some elk burger to spare. Daniel lived only half a mile down the road and the storekeeper said I can use the bike.

I jumped on the bike and pedaled down the road. About halfway there I met Daniel and his brother, who was visiting from Ohio. They were walking up the road to a pasture where some beef cows were. Daniel was originally from Ohio, and he had lived in Rexford for four years now. It happened that his family had come to visit right at the time. I asked Daniel if he would have some elk burger to spare. He seemed thrilled with the idea to share some of his burger.

I visited awhile yet with him and his brothers. He had a brother Robert, who lived in Rexford too. Soon another bachelor came along on his bike and stopped to talk. Next thing it was almost dark and I still hadn't gotten the burger.

Daniel finally went with me to the house trailer that he lived in and gave me a two-pound pack of elk burger out of his freezer. His parents were there so I visited with his father yet. Daniel had given me a plastic bag to carry the burger in. I hung it on the handlebars of the bike on my way back. But that didn't work well, for the bag rubbed against the wheel. When I had gone a ways the frozen meat fell through the bag and landed on the ground with a clatter. I stopped, wrapped the meat in the bag the best I could, and pedaled back to the store.

When I came to the store, it was closed and the other guys had gone back to the cabin. It was almost dark and I walked to the cabin alone, hoping there aren't any mountain lions waiting for an unarmed fellow with some tasty elk burger to pounce on.

I had just heard the story of the guy (right there in Rexford) who was trimming grass with a weed whacker, when he spied a mountain lion crouching behind him. The way I heard it the lion tried to attack him and he fended it off with the weed whacker. But I got to the cabin safely without seeing so much as a domestic cat.

I put the elk in the fridge for the next day. Now it was time to get some rest and a hot shower felt wonderful. It was past eleven o'clock when I finally sank into the bed that was to be my own for the next three nights. It was luxurious after three nights of trying to sleep on a crowded train—or in a hostel with other people—to have my own room with a good bed to sleep in. ZZZZZ...

Saturday morning, July 18, I slept until 8:30. I got up feeling refreshed and hungry. It was a cool morning with temperatures in the upper forties. A sweater felt good on the walk to the buffet for breakfast. The hot breakfast was tops. These home-cooked meals were spoiling us and I could see that this restaurant would be a popular eating place for the bachelors that lived in the area.

After breakfast we went back to the cabin. There was a sign at the driveway beside our cabin driveway that pointed to a secondhand store up on the hill behind our cabin. For want of anything better to do I went to check it out.

A lady by the name of Joyce Oaks lived there; her husband had died a year or so before, and she was trying to get rid of some of her stuff. She had a lot of old books, glassware and china, and she sold tea. I found a book about Obama that I thought looked interesting, and I bought some Linden Flower and Chamomile Lavender tea. The Chamomile lavender tea I thought might be a good thing to take along hiking to brew in the evening after a hard day of hiking. Chamomile is a good relaxant.

Joyce was an interesting woman. She lived on four acres by herself. There were three small cabins, a small greenhouse, a roofed area where the local school kept some auction things and a sheep pen where she kept sheep in that she had just bought. She had bought the sheep to try and clean up the weeds, and she also had chickens. She owned another home in Trego, Montana, and she had bought some property in Belize not long before. We visited awhile, and she showed me around the property. It was a nice property, but I wondered how long she would want to live there by herself. I guessed her to be in her upper sixties or lower seventies.

Right next door was a sawmill and a furniture shop that was run by the family whose name was Yoder. I thanked Joyce for the tea and for showing me around, then went to check out the sawmill and furniture shop. They built rustic furniture out of pine logs.

The shop seemed to be deserted when I entered. The doors were wide open, and I guessed that they never locked up anything, even on weekends. Probably the only need to close the doors would be to keep out the cold, or maybe bears and mountain lions. The property was set back in the woods and I could imagine there were wild animals around.

I walked around the shop looking at the machinery. Then I found the showroom and admired some of the nifty furniture they created. I imagined having this furniture in my own house and how nice it would look to have a whole set of this rustic design in my room. But when I started checking the prices and imagining the cost to ship this stuff for two thousand miles, I felt that if I want it that bad I might as well move to Rexford first. That way I could not only enjoy the nice furniture but also the mountains, scenery, and wildlife that goes with it. Much wishful thinking, but dreaming can be entertaining. You never know what could happen. If we would never dream, life would be mighty dull even if only five percent of our dreams come true. But the five percent that do come true is what makes life worthwhile.

As I was poking around in the shop, one of the boys that lived there came in the shop. We began talking about how we planned to hike in the Bob Marshall Wilderness and the fishing we planned to do. I guessed him to be in his upper teens. He talked about how the Koocanusa Lake and Glacier Park had good fishing. We had planned to hike down to the Koocanusa Lake that afternoon and he told me that a good place to fish is where Young's Creek empties into the lake.

The Koocanusa Lake was named to honor the Kootenai Indians, Canada, and the United States of America. The "Koo" stood for Kootenai, the "can: for Canada, and "usa" for the USA.

I bought a book from the boy that was written by an old bachelor whose name is Andrew Keim. The title of his book is Bears, Bucks, and Pack Rats. Andrew used to live in Rexford in his younger days but moved back to Ohio when he became older. He still goes to Rexford to visit and usually stays in a small cabin that is on the Yoder property when he visits. A boxful of these books was in the Yoder's showroom, and I thought they looked interesting. Andrew was an avid hunter in his younger days and hunted all kinds of big game. He got himself into many scrapes and hair-raising adventures on his hunting trips. A lot of his adventures are in the book now and can be enjoyed on a cold winter day beside the fire in an easy chair.

I went back to our cabin and washed my clothes that I had worn on the train. We went through our fishing gear one final time and weighed our packs. As I remember it, Elam's pack weighed seventy-five pounds, mine weighed sixty-four pounds, and Mervin beat us all at fifty-eight pounds. Elam and I both thought we were too heavy so we took a little this and some of that out of our packs. There wasn't a whole lot that we were willing to do without, and when we were done his pack weighed only three pounds less, mine was two pounds less and we weren't even carrying water yet! A full water bladder weighed six to seven pounds more. Oh well, we were going to do this somehow. There was no way one of us was backing out now.

I felt the best thing to do is sleep over it so I took a luxurious Saturday afternoon nap. I woke up refreshed and hungry.

We cooked up a scrumptious meal of elk burger, chicken noodle soup, and popcorn in the middle of the afternoon. With our stomachs full, we hiked the two miles to Koocanusa Lake and found where Young's Creek emptied into the lake.

It was a beautiful sunny day. The sky was clear blue, and the sun shone down warmly. There were a few boats out in the lake but the spot where we were we had to ourselves for a while.

But the fish weren't biting. I tried different flies that I thought looked good, but I didn't get any fish—only a few half-hearted nibbles. How I wished for some of those fat, wriggly, eastern night crawlers.

And then it happened. A small boat came along with three or four boys in it who were fishing. One of the boys was the Yoder boy whom I had met earlier that morning. They were catching small fish with night crawlers. I called out and asked if they would have any extra night crawlers. They threw me a box of a dozen, and I immediately put one on my hook. I caught a few small ones then, but nothing worth keeping for a meal. At least I was fishing in Montana and we had again experienced true Rexford hospitality.

We saw many different kinds of birds; most of them we don't have in the east. There were western tanagers, western sandpipers, ravens, and others we didn't identify.

The sun had set when we started back, and it cooled down fast. It was amazing how fast it cooled off with the low humidity. Even though the temperature could be in the nineties in the daytime, it always cooled off enough at night that it was no problem to sleep. In fact, a blanket felt good, and in the morning we turned on the heater. Heat in July seemed odd, but then, this was Montana.

On the two-mile hike back to the cabin we saw herds of mule deer and whitetail feasting on the irrigated hay fields. As a fellow farmer, I could easily imagine the damage they do. But it seemed like out there it just was a part of farming. If a farmer irrigated he was going to have deer in his fields.

It was dark when we came back to the cabin. After four days of travelling and settling in, the hike felt wonderful. I was becoming worried that I might get soft before we even started in the real wilderness.

I washed my clothes before I went to bed and hung them out to dry for Monday morning. It was 11:15 p.m. when I scribbled the day's happenings in my journal. I sank into the good bed that I called mine around midnight. It had been an interesting day, and I liked Rexford.

Sunday morning we got up, made a good breakfast of pancakes, bacon, toast, and cereal. Church services started at 9:00 and we had plenty of time to walk the quarter mile to church.

It was another beautiful morning with clear skies, cool, but not as cool as the last few mornings.

There was a busload of visitors from Indiana at church so it seemed like a large church. Being two thousand miles from home, visiting a church where the people spoke the same Pennsylvania Dutch dialect as we do at home (although the accent was different) was a very uplifting experience.

Church was held in a shed out of the sun's hot rays. Outside the sun shone hot but in the shed it was cool, another phenomenon of the low humidity. Back east if the sun shines that bright we can expect to sweat a lot in a shed like this at church. But the low humidity in the west made all the difference for it was comfortable in the shed.

Everybody filed in and sat down on the wooden benches, just like we do in the East.

The singing in the shed that morning was awesome. They sing a couple of octaves higher than what we are used to, and the sound reverberated through the shed. My spine tingled as I listened and helped sing the same German songs out of the same Ausbund we use at home. The Ausbund is the oldest Christian hymnal in the world that is still in continuous use. The mountain setting, the friendly people who shared the same faith (even if most of them were complete strangers) made me thankful for the privilege to participate in the services that morning.

The ministers who preached the sermons that morning were from Indiana. They preached inspiring and uplifting sermons. The scriptures for the sermon were Luke 15 and 16.

One minister spoke about asking and you shall receive. I couldn't help but think of how we got the elk burger. I had the urge to turn around to see if Daniel Mast was listening, but of course I didn't. I thought of how if I wouldn't have asked him I never would have gotten any burger. How often in life do we not get what we wish for just because we don't ask? Jesus himself tells us to ask anything in His name and we shall receive. Very deep things to ponder about.

After the sermon everybody kneeled in prayer; then there was more of that wonderful singing and the service was over. The two and a half hours of worship seemed short, but it was refreshing to our souls. Just like the good food we had for our bodies here in Rexford, so we were fed spiritual nourishment for our souls. Something everyone needs to be satisfied and at peace.

After church we went back to our cabin and enjoyed the rest of the elk burger. Before it was time to go back for supper I took a nap and wrote some postcards to send back home on Monday morning.

Later in the afternoon, we walked back to where church had been to play volleyball and eat supper. It was great getting around with the Rexford young folks and playing volleyball to loosen our soft muscles. It seemed all we did that week was sit around, eat, sleep, and get fat. With all the training we had done before the trip and now, a week of not doing much, I was almost certain that I was gaining a few pounds. But I was sure once we were in the wilderness the extra pounds would burn off.

With eighteen bachelors living in Rexford at the time, we felt right at home with them. We had good volleyball games, and the girls that were helping played well, too. It was a great experience, being so far from home yet feeling like we were among friends.

We played volleyball for a while until the call came for supper. This time we had a haystack meal. Again, I marveled at how well these folks could cook.

No offense to the Lancaster County cooks because there are excellent cooks in Lancaster County, too. Maybe it was the mountain air, maybe it was the friendly people, or the pretty girls; whatever it was, the food was delicious.

After supper we visited awhile, played more volleyball, then sang for about an hour. We sang German hymns for half an hour then English. The first song we sang in English was "God Moves in a Mysterious Way," one of my favorite songs. It touched me deeply, singing this song here in Montana, far from home among other believers and likeminded people. When I thought of the situation and events leading to this trip, God indeed moves in a mysterious way.

At 9:00 the singing ended. There was an hour of light left so we played more volleyball. I had figured out who Cindy Miller was and now I decided it was time to give her the hello that her Uncle Ammon Yoder had sent. I was nervous about it; I had never met this girl before and I didn't know how well a Montana girl would appreciate it to have a complete stranger from the East to approach her. At least her boyfriend came from Pennsylvania so I hoped she wouldn't be offended.

It happened that I played on the same team that Cindy was on and when it became too dark to play I figured it is now or never. As she walked away from the net I approached her and said, "Someone told me that you are Cindy Miller."

She looked at me and I figured she probably felt like saying, "Who are you?" And I didn't blame her.

I quickly explained my mission, how I had met her uncle on the train and he asked me to say hello. When she heard her uncle's name she softened up and we had an interesting conversation. She asked me if I knew any Fishers from Pennsylvania. I told her I was aware that she is dating a fellow by the name of Ben Fisher, but no, "I didn't know him."

We had a good talk for about ten or fifteen minutes. We talked about how nice it is in Rexford, that she teaches school as a helper, the hockey games they play in the wintertime, what we planned to do in the wilderness and so on. It was neat that I could pass on the hello like that and I was glad that I mustered up the courage to approach her. She was a good conversationalist, something I found to be true with a lot of the people there. I guess if a person moves that far away from home and likes it, they cannot be shy.

At 10:30 it was dark and we decided it is time to return to our cabin for the night. The next day we were heading for the great Bob Marshall Wilderness.

We got up at 4:30 the next morning and cooked a delicious breakfast of pancakes, toast, and bacon. Our last home-cooked meal for two weeks.

Mike was there at 6:00 (just like he had promised) to take us on the three-hour ride south. We loaded our heavy packs and suitcases, which quite filled up the back of the suburban he was driving.

Leaving the cabin and Rexford gave me a twinge of sadness as I thought about all the nice people we had met, the good food, the comfortable cabin, and the mountains. But we were headed for the wilderness where there was more mountains and adventure. Rexford will always have a special place in my heart, and if the opportunity ever presents itself again, I will be back.

# Chapter Three:
# Climbing Mountains and Blisters

We stopped in Kalispell at the post office to ship our luggage to Fairfield at Dave's house. Elam knew Dave from the previous trip he had done when Dave had hiked with them three years before. We had planned for Dave to pick us up at the trail's end at Gibson Reservoir on the east side of the wilderness. Now we had only our packs with us.

We stopped at a Wal-Mart to get a small pan and the olive oil to cook our fish in. We bought the lightest pan we could find that was big enough, then took the handle off to save weight and space. Finally we were all set and headed for the great Bob Marshall Wilderness!

With all the stops we made it took until 11:00 A.M. to reach the Pyramid Pass trailhead. When we reached the parking lot at the trailhead Elam looked around at us and asked if anyone wants to bail out yet. This was our last chance, because once we were on the trail, turning back was not a good option. Nobody seemed to be interested so Mike left.

Other than a couple vehicles, the parking lot was deserted. Already the peaceful stillness of the wilderness could be felt, although the official wilderness was four or five miles up to Pyramid Pass.

Now we were finally ready for the real thing. After months of training and preparation, to actually be at the trailhead ready to hike seemed a little unreal. But there was no denying the fact that we were here so we divided the gallon of water we brought along, strapped our packs onto our backs and headed up to Pyramid Pass. We had only gone a few hundred yards when we met a horse and rider leading another horse down the trail. He nodded at us, looked at our packs, and said, "You guys look like you are packed pretty heavy." We agreed.

It was a 2100 foot climb to the top of Pyramid Pass. The trail was good, but it was a relentless ascent.

*Entering the Bob Marshall Wilderness Complex*
*at Flathead National Forest on top of Pyramid Pass.*

About a mile up the trail we came to a huckleberry patch. I feasted on huckleberries for a while. Elam and Mervin went on.

Almost at the top I caught up with Elam and Mervin at a small lake where we tried our fishing gear. We had a few bites but no catches.

At the top we came to a sign that said we are entering the Bob Marshall Wilderness. It had been a long climb. Five miles of uphill hiking with loaded packs had made me ready to look for a campsite at Pyramid Lake that was supposed to be up there somewhere.

We walked on, but somewhere we missed the side trail that led to Pyramid Lake. We hiked on down the other side for another two and a half miles until we came to a beautiful spot called Leota Park. Leota Park is a campsite that has corrals and hitching rails for outfitters that travel through. It was a great spot, nestled in a valley beside a cold stream with Leota Peak towering to the north of us with its highest point jagging into the sky at 8512 feet. We camped in a meadow at the bottom of an avalanche slide. We could see where the snow slid off the mountains and tore up trees by their roots.

Coming down from Pyramid Pass with my loaded pack did a number to my feet. I had noticed that my feet had a few hot spots, but when I took my shoes and socks off I was shocked to see a couple small white blisters on my feet. We were camped right next to the clear, cold stream. The first thing I did was soak my feet in the cold water. The water was ice cold and my feet soon cooled off.

It had been a hard day. Getting up at 4:30, hiking up the mountain and down again had about done us in for the first day. We hiked seven and a half miles that day. But the scenery was wild and beautiful. We saw western grouse, chipmunks, brown squirrels, and gophers. We camped right beside a colony of gophers. They didn't seem very happy to share their headquarters with us, but we had no inclination to move because of them.

For supper I had a bagel with peanut butter and honey, beef-flavored Ramen noodles, and a hot cup of that good tea with honey I had bought at Rexford.

I was sore from the heavy pack, and by 9:00 I was ready to retire for the night, although it wasn't dark yet. In this area we weren't allowed campfires; we had cooked our food on our stoves and there was no fire to sit around.

When we came to the campsite and plopped down our packs, Elam remarked, "It feels like I did a hard day's work." I couldn't have agreed with him more and I was glad for every bit of training I had done. In fact, I wished I would have put even more effort in. I hoped I would become stronger and harder in the next few days.

At 9:00 P.M. I stretched out in my tent and fell asleep. About an hour later something woke me. I opened my tent fly, peered out cautiously, and there was a herd of around fifteen elk grazing two hundred yards off. It wasn't quite dark yet so I watched them through my binoculars for a while. They spooked from me when I opened the tent fly and ran off a little. Then the herd bull bellowed out a long, loud bugle. It was a wild, awesome sound that reverberated in the valley that we were in. They stayed around all night and we could hear the cows calling back and forth to their calves throughout the night. In the morning the bull bugled again at daybreak. Writing about that bugle still gives me the chills.

When we got up, the elk left, went running up the ridge beside Leota peak and were soon gone. It was amazing how the elk with calves by their sides could run right up the steep ridge in no time. We figured it would make a difference to have four legs.

A robin's notes were the first of the birds I heard that morning. There were other birds too that I couldn't name, and I wished for a western bird book. But a bird book would have added weight. I enjoyed the music anyway.

It was a gorgeous morning. The sun hadn't come up over the mountains yet when I stepped out of my tent. The sky was cloudless, and at forty-three degrees it was chilly.

A jackrabbit had hopped into camp and was having breakfast on some greens about fifty yards away. The gophers popped out of their dens and rudely stared at us, wishing we would go away. I tossed a few rocks at them and watched them pop back into their holes.

Breakfast consisted of granola cereal with dried milk and hot water poured on it. I ate it right out of the Ziploc bag with my spork. A spork is a spoon with teeth on the end to use as a fork. Some sporks have a spoon on one end of the handle with a fork on the other end. Mine had its teeth at the end of the spoon. Hence the name spork.

A stick of string cheese, a hot cup of Swiss Miss, and my protein shake finished breakfast. For lunch I packed Dove candy, almonds, dried fruit, beef jerky, string cheese, and granola bars. We filtered water from the cold stream and began packing up.

My blisters were sore from the previous day. I wore two pairs of socks for more cushion.

We packed up and decided to hike up Leota Peak. At 8512 feet it stuck up into the sky 2100 feet higher than the trail. We hung our packs on a down tree close to the trail, took our water bottles along, and since there was no trail to the top we had to bushwhack.

It was a steep, tough climb. We picked our way up through a wash that was cut in the side of the mountain. We were headed for the east side of the mountain where it looked like it wouldn't be quite as steep to the top. But when we got up higher there was a ledge running along towards the west side that we decided looked a little easier.

Elam was leading the way and when the ledge narrowed down to a foot or so wide I chickened out. On top of the ledge the cliffs went straight up, and below there was steep shale that slid down toward the valley. Mervin had chickened out awhile back and was quite a ways behind us. Elam had gone on around so I rested on a large flat area of rock.

We had ascended about 1500 feet from where we started, and the air was thinner. At first I couldn't figure out why I had to puff so much when we only climbed twenty or thirty feet up at a time. Then I decided for us flatlanders that are used to six or seven hundred feet above sea level, this 8000 foot elevation would be quite a difference.

Elam disappeared around the ledge, and I sat there for a while enjoying the view. I was alone and the stillness was incredible. The lack of sound in the wilderness can be felt rather than heard. The country around me was so vast that I felt like a tiny speck in it.

Sitting there for a while rested me, and soon it bothered me that I wasn't at the top. I looked to the east and saw a crevice going up through the cliffs between huge boulders. I decided to work my way over there, but there was steep shale I had to cross first.

I sat there for a while, drinking in the view. A bird that resembled an eastern bluebird was flying nearby among the rocks. Since we were in the West I assumed it was a western bluebird.

Finally it bothered me that I wasn't at the top. I set out across the steep shale. Taking my water bladder along I picked my way across. When I got to the crevice in the rocks I had to scramble to get up. It was so steep I wondered who would find me if I fell. It was more of that slippery shale and one misstep could be a broken leg, a twisted ankle, or worse… I tried not to think about it.

I was panting hard when I got through the crevice, but I wasn't even close to the top. I still had about 500 feet to go with another two to three hundred feet of elevation gain. It wasn't quite as steep there, so I picked my way up, stopping often to catch my breath. But then it became steeper and suddenly I came to a crack in the rocks that was about two feet wide, fifty feet long, and twelve feet deep. In the middle there was a dark hole about four feet long that the bottom couldn't be seen. On the other side of the crack were more cliffs that looked worse than what I just came up. Right there I chickened out again. I'd rather be a live dog than a dead lion.

I sat there on the rocks for a while, resting and drinking in the view. To my left, way down, was Crimson Lake and when I lifted my eyes, all I could see was mountain range after mountain range with no sign of any kind of civilization. There wasn't as much as a trail to where I was, and this was some of the wildest country I had ever seen.

*From Leota Peak looking down into Crimson Lake.*

Suddenly I heard a yell in the distance that echoed around the mountains. "Must be Elam made it to the top," I thought. At least I hoped that is all it was about. Then everything was silent, and I felt alone in that wild country again.

I sat there a bit longer trying to grasp the vastness, the beauty, the wildness, the silence, and the actual atmosphere I was in. It was hard to grasp that I was in a pristine wilderness, living a dream that few people get to realize. Viewing God's handiwork from this height and mulling over the circumstances that led to this trip made me realize anew that our Creator's ways are past finding out.

But as all mountaintop experiences go, we must eventually head down to the valley again. Of course I hadn't quite made it to the top but at least I was alive and well. My Gatorade in my water bladder was about gone and I had a long, steep descent ahead of me.

When I was coming up the crevice on the slippery shale I had decided I will not go down on that route. I circled around towards the north and picked my way down to the ridge that the elk had crossed that morning.

From the top the ridge hadn't looked as steep, but it still was a long, steep descent down once I reached the ridge.

I had picked my way down to about where I had last seen Elam when I met Mervin. He hadn't made it close to the top and wondered where Elam was. I told him I hadn't seen him for a while but I did hear a shout when I was up there. Mervin had heard it too and we hoped he was okay. Mervin went around to the west edge as far as he dared without seeing Elam. The mountain was so huge that trying to find someone on foot on the steep slopes seemed hopeless. We picked our way down the wash where we came up and I told Mervin to just watch, probably Elam found another way down and would be waiting for us at the trail. I tried not to think about what we would do if we came to the trail and he wouldn't show up for a couple hours. But I knew Elam was in top physical condition, and I knew him well enough to know that he could be very independent.

We picked our way down the steep slope and after a while I left Mervin behind. He had injured his foot during training, and it slowed him down when he was descending.

I was about halfway down and had dropped down about fifteen feet into a gully when I heard a noise to my right above me and coming towards me. I knew we were in bear country so I stopped and looked up and over to my right. Soon a beautiful muledeer buck came trotting along above me. He didn't see me until he was directly above me no more than fifteen feet away. When he saw me he stopped and stared as if to say, "Who are you and what do you want here?" We stared at each other until he had seen enough. He circled around me and went trotting easily away across the mountain. For a moment I wished I had four legs. His antlers had eight points with at least a twenty-inch spread and his rack stood way above his head. The antlers still had velvet on them. He was awesome, and I was thankful for the privilege to see such a magnificent animal up close.

# Chapter Three: Climbing Mountains and Blisters

I picked my way down to where we had left our packs and waited for Mervin to catch up. He was soon with me and as we were wondering where Elam was he came walking down the trail from Leota Park to us, looking none the worse. We were relieved to see him. He said that once he had gone around the ledge where I had chickened out, the mountain had leveled out a little and he had made it to the top. When he got to the top, he had yelled in triumph that Mervin and I had heard. On the way down he had found another wash that was easier than the one we went and had brought him on the trail farther west of our campsite.

Since we all had whistles, we agreed to set up signals when we got separated and couldn't find each other. One whistle meant "where are you," and three whistles in a row meant an emergency where someone needed immediate assistance. We hoped nobody would ever need to whistle three times. But the mountains in the wilderness are unforgiving, and it is good to be prepared.

The trail that day wasn't as steep and went around the base of Crimson Peak to a ford on Young's creek.

Soon after we were on the trail again from Leota Peak, we met a group of hikers who said they had been in the wilderness for twenty-one days. Apparently they hadn't packed all their food for twenty-one days because their packs didn't look like they would hold that much.

At the ford by Young's Creek it felt good to peel off my socks and wade across in my sandals. My feet were bothering me, and by the end of the day I realized it was a mistake to wear two pairs of socks. It gave me extra cushion, but they made my feet too hot.

We had hiked eleven miles with the climb up Leota Peak and were camped along Young's Creek just below Young's Falls.

We saw a little wildlife. I saw a bird that looked like a PA grouse but had only a short tail. It was taking a dust bath on the trail and sat there until I was almost on it before it walked into the woods. It acted like a tame chicken so I figured it was either a prairie chicken or a western grouse. At camp we saw an osprey and other birds I couldn't name.

By Tuesday night I had given my pack a name. I called it "The Klutz." He was holding up well so far. But I noticed he had started creaking that day. In fact, I couldn't blame him for creaking like that because by the end of the second day my whole body felt all creaky. I hoped that as the trip wore on I would be able to consider the Klutz to be a friend instead of a burden. He definitely had a knack of keeping my gear together, something I greatly appreciated.

We pitched our tents beside Young's creek where we could hear the soothing sound of running water to lull ourselves to sleep.

At 9:00 I went in my tent, made an entry in my journal, doctored my blistered feet and crashed. The cold bath I had taken in the creek earlier had soothed my blisters and refreshed me a great deal.

Elam had gone fishing, and as darkness was settling in he came back with a single fish. It was too small for the three of us. Since I was in my tent already, I didn't get any after he had it cooked. He shared with Mervin though, and by the sound of things it was worth eating. I hoped we would have the privilege to catch some more.

But now it was nap time and the air beside the creek was becoming chilly. I burrowed into my warm sleeping bag, sank down on my sleeping mat and feel asleep, listening to the gentle sound of water flowing over the rocks through the pristine, pine forest.

That night I awoke around 12:00 and stepped outside of my tent to answer the call of nature. There was no moon and as I looked up at the clear night sky I was treated to an incredible display of stars. It was nothing like we ever see in the East. The stars were so bright I could see by their light. There were stars everywhere, right down to the horizon. My first impression was that I'm seeing lights on the horizon but then I discovered that it was stars. Then there was the Milky Way. It looked like a cloudy film with layers upon layers of stars stacked on top of each other with no sign of any kind of man-made light around.

The sky was vast and there was again that incredible stillness. My heart was touched deep inside where it seldom gets touched. I wished I could somehow take the scene home and share it with the folks in the East that never had, and probably never will, see something like this.

I thought of the time that God called Abraham out to count the stars and Abraham couldn't do it. And then God told him that his descendents will be like the stars in heaven. I thought of how we read in Psalms 147 that God counts the number of stars and calls them all by name. And I wondered, "If God is so big and creates something so vast, why would He ever listen to mere man? Who are we to ask Him for favors?" But a person doesn't have to read far in the Bible to realize our God cares about us humans and loves us no matter how often we fail and feel unloved.

## Chapter Three: Climbing Mountains and Blisters

As I entered my tent again and burrowed into my warm sleeping bag, I tried to think of the right word to describe what I had just seen and experienced. The only word I could think of was AWESOME in capital letters. Even awesome feels like a frail word to use. Our God is too big to describe Him with mere words.

# Chapter Four:
# Hiking Along Young's Creek

Wed., July 22, the third day of our hike we woke up to overcast skies. The temperature was forty-one degrees and it spritzed a little, then cleared off. It cooled off some and didn't get quite as hot as the two previous days.

We had breakfast, packed up camp and forded Young's Creek where the trail crossed it. Most of the creek crossings we had to wade across. We all had water shoes or sandals that we wore across the streams to protect our feet from sharp rocks and to keep them from slipping and pitching us in the ice cold water.

I was the first to hit the trail that morning. I crossed Young's creek, took my sandals off, and let my feet dry before putting my socks and shoes on again. The cold water felt good to my blisters. I had covered the blisters with duct tape, which helped to relieve the chafing. Duct tape works like a second skin. One thing sure, never again was I going to wear two pairs of socks to cushion blisters.

Soon after I got on the trail again, I came upon a whitetail doe grazing beside the trail. She didn't spook much at all and went right on eating at about fifteen yards off as I passed her.

Shortly afterward the trail crossed Young's Creek again. Now Young's Creek was on our right. We stayed on trail number 141 along Young's Creek and kept looking for fishing holes. I couldn't wait to catch my first fish and have it for lunch.

The trail was fairly level along the creek with Gordon Mountain on our left, with a peak at 8368 feet. Young's Creek was on our right then Jumbo

Mountain stretched up to 8284 feet above sea level. Gordon Mountain rose more gradually on the west side of the trail while Jumbo Mountain rose sharply to the east.

The trail was at 5000 feet, and the Jumbo Mountain cliffs were sheer and plunged down thousands of feet to the river. It was spectacular and very wild. One place there was a spot about a thousand feet up that was called the Hole in the Wall Cave. It was a great hole, right into the face of the cliff. It looked interesting, but unless you were a cliff climber there was no way to reach that hole.

We followed the trail along Young's Creek to where the creek slowed down to pools of water that looked like fish would be there. The trail had switched to number 125.

*Trail through cool, pine forest.*

A short side trail led us through the pines to the creek where I dropped the Klutz, put on my water shoes, assembled my fly rod and tied on a fly. I cast the fly and waited for a bite. The fish were biting, and after a few casts I caught an eleven-inch trout. I was so excited I felt like jumping up and down and shouting. This was my first fish in the great Bob Marshall Wilderness!

There was no way I was going to let this one get away. I set a rock on top of it and resumed fishing

As usual Elam had wandered off by himself, leaving just Mervin and I at this wonderful spot. Mervin had a few bites and he drifted a little downstream. As I was there casting different flies with the sun shining brightly, the wildness of it all, again, touched the spot in my heart that seldom gets touched. It was almost surreal, the way the wilderness kept touching me like it was trying to say something and I couldn't quite understand what it was saying. I have yet to figure out which words to use to adequately describe the vastness and the depth of a wilderness experience. In fact, I doubt such words exist.

Then something happened that drove home the reality of having to make do with what you have. I was casting across the creek into a deep pool under some branches, where I was certain trout resided, when my hook caught on the bushes. Being the greenhorn I was and having caught one trout already I thought I knew something about it. I tried jerking the rod back and forth but still the hook was caught fast. Then I gave it a good jerk that bent my rod in a large arc. Suddenly I heard a sickening snap and my rod went limp. I learned the hard way that fly rods are very sensitive and will break much sooner than the spinning reels I had used since childhood. There I was with a broken fly rod in my hands, with the closest fly shop a two days' hike out of the wilderness. Now I would experience the part of the wilderness where I would need to depend on my own ingenuity and the supplies that I had, to deal with what the wilderness dealt me and the predicament of my own inexperience with fly rods.

I had packed a roll of ten to twelve feet of duct tape in the Klutz so I pulled that out and proceeded to repair the fly rod with good ole duct tape that has a thousand uses for it. The rod had broken about two feet from the tip where a splice was. I trimmed the broken edges a little, stuck it together, wrapped it tightly with duct tape, and went back to fishing.

By that time the fish had figured out that a greenhorn was on the banks and quit biting. I cast a few more times but it was no use. I packed my gear, pulled on my shoes, packed the fish in the Klutz, shouldered the Klutz on my back, and hiked down the trail to the next campsite.

On the way to the next campsite we went through a lot of places where there had been forest fires in the years gone by. It was much hotter in those areas, and on a bright sunny day it became uncomfortably warm compared to the shady forest. The burned areas were anywhere from two to twenty years old. In this drier climate there is much competition for moisture, and the regrowth is much slower than in the East.

The trees were mostly lodge pole pine with an occasional clump of ponderosas. The lodge pole pine is an interesting tree. In the West they have learned that fighting forest fires in an old timber stand is hard on it. The lodge pole pine has a cone that only germinates in extreme heat. As long as the wildfires are not endangering any dwellings they let them burn. This allows old forests new regrowth that enhances the ecosystem. In some areas the trails went through regrowth that was about ten years old and the new regrowth was thick enough that I felt we probably aren't in any danger from bears in those areas. The trees were so thick I wondered if a rabbit even lived there.

The trees averaged about ten feet high and in a few years they would thin out because there was not enough of moisture for them to all survive. In the

*Thick regrowth of lodgepole pines.*

wilderness only the strongest and fittest survive, be it man, beast, or plants.

We came together and were looking for a camping spot when we came to an area where there were a lot of down trees and Young's Creek made a sharp turn close to the trail. The pool at the bend looked like it would hold fish so we unpacked our fly rods and fished for a while. I caught another smaller one, and we had a total of four fish for supper.

We found a beautiful campsite beside Young's Creek about a half mile farther than the deep pool, just above where Young's Creek flows into the South Fork of the Flathead river. With all the fishing we had done we still had hiked 7.3 miles that day.

We cleaned the fish and fried them in the small pan in olive oil on our small stoves. They tasted like no other fish I ever had before. Once they were cooked we spritzed a little salt on them, peeled the meat off of the bones, and ate them right on the spot. Few things I have ever eaten tasted better than those fish. I don't know it if was the mountain air, the beautiful campsite, the clean flat rocks we used for plates, or the fact that we were hungry that made it the best fish-eating experience I have ever had. My mouth still waters when I think of those fish. I suppose the fresh mountain streams that we caught them in contributed to the flavor too. The water is some of the purest and cleanest water on earth. Eating fish that we caught ourselves was one of the best wilderness experiences we had, and ranked at the top.

A whitetail doe came and snooped around our camp and came within thirty yards until we spooked her away.

For a snack after the fish I opened a Dove candy chocolate where it said on the wrapper, "Give yourself the day off." I felt like I had done a hard day's work. We had hiked over seven miles, caught fish, plus I had carried one fish almost half a day and the Klutz still wasn't much lighter than when we started. In fact, it probably weighed as much as when I started with the fish I carried. I didn't intend to carry fish again. Next time, I would cook them on the spot.

At 9:00 I wearily crawled into my tent, set my bear spray within arm's reach, doctored my blistered feet, made an entry into my journal, snuggled into my sleeping bag, and with the sweet memory of the fish we had eaten I drifted off in slumberland.

At around 2:30 A.M. I was awakened by something sniffing and walking around outside my tent. I thought about bears and lay there hoping it would go away. It didn't go away. I grabbed my flashlight, unzipped my tent and shone around. It was pitch dark. I shone around in the darkness among the trees until I saw the glare of a wild animal's eyes about forty yards off. It was only a mule deer. At 4:00 another one sniffed around outside my tent. I left that one go.

At 5:30 I got up feeling refreshed. Sleeping in the mountain air does marvelous good to the mind, body, and soul.

I hiked back to the deep pool to try and catch some fish for breakfast. I caught two smaller fish and had those for breakfast. A wonderful way to start the day.

At forty-nine degrees in the morning it was the warmest morning yet. The sky was overcast; it looked like it could rain on the fourth day of our hike. It did spritz a little but didn't amount to much.

A short distance from camp on the trail, we came across fresh bear tracks in the dust. It made us realize that we truly are in bear country, although we still hadn't seen any.

# Chapter Five:
# Fishing the South Fork of the Flathead

A little farther on we came to where Young's Creek flowed into the south Fork of the Flathead River. Now we were ready for some real fishing.

The South Fork of the Flathead River is a beautiful river that winds though the heart of the Bob Marshall Wilderness and eventually empties into the Hungry Horse reservoir. It has some of the best fishing in the whole wilderness area. The Hungry Horse Reservoir dam keeps a lot of the big predator fish from travelling upstream; therefore, the cutthroat trout have a better chance to be more plentiful.

The river flows through some of the most remote and wildest country a person can find in the Lower Forty-Eight. There are deep, clear pools at the bends that hold oodles of trout where you can see them ten feet down or more. The largest cutthroats we caught were fourteen to sixteen inches. Then there was the coveted bull trout that grow up to thirty inches long.

The bull trout are an endangered species, and we had to have special catch cards that allowed us to even fish for them. In that area bull trout all have to be released. There is only one section of the wilderness area where they allow you to keep two bull trout a year, but we were not in that area.

Now we were on trail number 125 and followed the river downstream on the west side. We were on the lookout for deep pools at the bends and fished a lot. I had two fish for breakfast so I threw them all back for I had no intention of packing any fish as we intended to camp near the river that night.

Elam soon found a hole and fished by himself most of the day while Mervin and I went to the next spot. We didn't go far until we saw where the river made a couple sharp turns about a quarter mile from the trail. It looked like a promising spot, but to get to it was a different story.

The area we were in had been burned a few years before and there was a tangled mass of logs to cross to get to the river. Anyone who has ever seen what it looks like in a burned area that is a couple years old knows how difficult it is to bushwhack through such an area. But we didn't come all the way out here and expect it to be easy. There is a reason the wilderness has such phenomenal fishing and we intended to make the most of it.

The trail was on the lower side of a steep hill. To get to the river we had to slide down about twenty feet, then cross the flat marshy area with the tangled deadfalls. The packs on our backs slowed us down and it took us about half an hour to get to the river.

We had no clue which flies to use so I just tied one on. At first we didn't catch much. I slipped on my water shoes and worked my way down the river until I came to a spot where there was a deep pool close to the bank on the other side of the river. There was a fallen tree out across the water, and I found that casting under those areas where trees or bushes hang out is where the fish hide. The fish were biting. After a bit I felt a tug on my line, strong enough that I knew it was more than just a six-incher. I hauled it in and it put up quite a fight.

When I had it in the shallow water my rod was bent into a J when suddenly there was a sickening snap and my rod went limp. My rod had broken where I had taped it the day before, but miraculously the line held. I reeled the fish in to where I could catch it with my hand before it could spit out the hook. It was a nice fourteen-inch cutthroat trout. Proudly I held it up, admiring its beauty, then I gently put it back into the water and watched it swim away among the rocks.

Mervin had gone to another hole and I felt alone there beside the river in that wild area. It was another true wilderness experience. My rod was broken, the sun was shining, the river kept on flowing and the silence was as loud as ever. Now I had to again deal with a broken rod, days from any fly shop. This time I did real surgery on my rod and took the time to do it right. After all, I had twelve days of wilderness to experience yet and time doesn't mean as much out there.

I took a green willow twig about a quarter inch in diameter from the many willows that were growing on the banks of the river. Then I took the precious roll of duct tape and wrapped the twig tightly onto the broken part of the rod. When I was done, the six-inch splint bent with the rod almost as good as new. I proudly surveyed my handiwork and went back to fishing. But all this had taken a great deal of time and the fish had quit biting. By now Mervin had come back. We packed up our gear and made our way across the tangled brush back to the trail.

With the new splint on my rod I couldn't take it apart completely because the break was right at a splice. Now I had about six inches of sensitive fly rod sticking out of the top of the Klutz. I would have to be careful that it wouldn't catch somewhere and break off completely.

We fished a lot that day and I lost count at around six fish. I had never been a big fan of catch and release, but I had never fished the Bob Marshall Wilderness before. Our limit to keep was three fish per day, and those had to be under twelve inches, except in the lakes. At the lakes there was no limit to the size of the fish we could keep.

Later in the afternoon a small thunderstorm kicked up and rained just enough to make us pull our covers over our packs and consider getting out our rain gear. The wind kicked up and a couple dead trees from forest fires come crashing down nearby. It made us realize that bears weren't the only danger we faced. In fact, bears were by far not the most dangerous thing to worry about in the wilderness.

The rain didn't amount to much but it cooled off a lot.

We set up camp at 6:30 right along the river by a good fishing hole.

My sleeping bag got washed that day. When I pulled it out of the Klutz I discovered that my drinking water bladder had been leaking, had soaked parts of my sleeping bag, and washed it for me. I threw it over a bush to dry, hoping the Montana air would dry it by bedtime.

We only hiked five miles with all the fishing we had done that day so the Klutz had a bit of a break. We were getting along with each other better than we were at first, although he still made me puff up the hills.

The wildlife in the area was plentiful. I saw a whitetail deer, a bald eagle, goldfinches, and the day before, hummingbirds. In camp three sandhill cranes came flying in with their singular cries and landed on a sandbar just up the river from the camp.

For supper I had some wild onions with my noodles. Elam had met a man on the trail who showed him what wild onions looked like. They grew in abundance in that area. They added a delicious fresh flavor to the drab taste of dried food.

The fish weren't biting so for supper I had no fish. I hoped by morning they would be biting.

At 10:10 P.M. I entered in my journal that my tent is smelling like a camping trip. The Montana air had almost dried my sleeping bag completely so at least I could sleep dry. But the smell was still there. There was no way around it and camping for days at a time without using soap produces scents that only come from camping for days at a time without using soap. But that was part of it. A freshly washed body and bedding every night wouldn't be a true wilderness experience. The smell never kept me from sleeping well, but rather, it probably helped me to sleep better.

Friday morning when I awoke it was clear and cold, around 40 degrees. I wiggled out of my cozy sleeping bag and went to catch a few fish for breakfast.

I caught two nice fish and with my granola cereal I had wild raspberries that we found beside the trail not far from camp. For once I was completely satisfied. It was neat harvesting wild food to supplement our trail food.

We hiked about a mile along the river until we came to a place called Big Prairie where the forest service had their head quarters for the area. Big Prairie is a large flat area with a hundred acres fenced in with rail and jackposts. Jackposts are A-shaped posts that you don't have to dig holes for. The A-shaped posts sit on the ground with rails on each side and one on the top where the cross is.

Inside the enclosure there were a cluster of cabins where the forest service and trail crews kept supplies. There is a person on duty all the time there, and he welcomed us into the main cabin where there was fresh Gatorade waiting for thirsty hikers. The shelves were stocked with a large supply of canned goods and other food.

One of the cabins was a bunkhouse where the trail crews slept when they were off duty. The forest service trail crews go out in pairs—for ten days at a time—to clear trails of fallen trees and brush. They use only hand tools like axes, saws, and knives. Chainsaws and any kind of motors are illegal in the wilderness area. Crews work on the trail for ten days, have four days off, then back on the trail for another ten days, all summer long.

The ranger showed us another cabin where the tools were kept. There was rope, axes, saws, hatchets and hand tools of every description. There were even crosscut saws that they still used. On the porch there was a jig that they used to sharpen the saws. The workshop cabin had a root cellar that the ranger showed us where they kept the perishables like bread. It was heavily insulated and felt cool.

Then he showed us the horse barn. They had corrals for the horses where the packers who came in with supplies kept their horses. In the barn there was hay, feed, saddles, and tack. Everything had to be hauled in on horseback or on foot.

It was like stepping back at least a hundred years in time. It was a quiet, peaceful place. There were tall mountains on each side, the beautiful Flathead River flowed through the valley, and there were no motors to disturb the singular silence.

While we were being showed around a party of riders from Rich Ranch Outfitters came riding into the area. The owner's name was Jack Rich. There were about ten people in the outfit, mostly older folks. They were riding and fishing in the wilderness and seemed to be having a good time.

We visited with them awhile then Jack quoted a saying about the wilderness that I'll probably never forget. He said, "When all is said and done it recharges the part that cannot be seen." Words cannot express what the wilderness did to my heart. The saying that Jack quoted is true.

When we were done touring the place, we went back across the river on the packbridge. Some of the main trails had packbridges across the river where the water was too deep to ford. A packbridge is a suspension bridge made of planks and beams, suspended by thick cables that are anchored down on each side. The bridges sway back and forth high above the water when they are crossed. Nevertheless, they are sturdily built and we didn't feel any danger when we crossed.

The trail was fairly level along the river. About a mile from Big Prairie we came to a spot where the river made a sharp bend and there was a deep fishing hole. The banks were about ten feet high and went almost straight down to the water. Banks or no banks, I was bound to get a fly into the water there. At the bottom there was a couple feet of level earth to stand on before the water.

I dropped my pack, pulled my gear out, and slid down the bank to where I could fish. I was not disappointed. I could see the fish swimming around in the pools of clear water.

The river was fairly wide where I was, and the water was only a couple feet

*The packbridge at Big Prairie.*

deep for about ten feet to where there was a ledge that dropped sharply into a very deep pool.

Elam didn't feel like coming down the steep bank so he went on to the next hole. Mervin hung around awhile, watching me fish.

I tied a fly on my rod and cast. I had a few bites where I could see the fish coming for the fly but no real hits.

Then I noticed a more shallow pool to my left where I could see a few fish swimming around. To reach the pool I had to go to the edge of the water where the ground was muddy and I had to really stretch out with my casts.

I cast a few times when bam, a fish hit so hard it almost pulled me into the water. I slipped and slid in the mud as I reeled the fish in, determined that this one was not getting away.

The fish put up quite a fight. When I finally landed it on the bank it was a nice fifteen-inch cutthroat. I took the hook out of its mouth and proudly held it up for Mervin to see, then released it back into the river and watched it swim away.

Mervin followed Elam to the next hole while I kept on fishing. I decided to try for bull trout. I got my spinning rod and tied on a big streamer. I got so wrapped up in trying to catch fish that I lost all track of time.

I didn't catch any bull trout, but I had a lot of fun trying.

When I got back on the trail and had hiked for a mile or so, I looked at my watch and was startled to see that it was 2:30 already. I learned time flies when a person is flyfishing. No pun intended.

At 3:30 I caught up with the other guys at a small stream where the trail crossed. Elam had washed his clothes and had them on a line to dry. It felt like a good time for lunch break so I sat down in the shade and enjoyed my lunch.

We hiked a few more miles until we came to a beautiful spot beside the river called Murphy Flats. There were large Ponderosa pines that we set up our tents under, and the river looked like it would hold fish.

The total mileage for that day was 11.8 miles.

We set up camp and went fishing. We caught a few, but I threw all mine back because I didn't think they were big enough. But then I didn't catch

*Large Ponderosa Pines*

anything bigger so I had to go without fish for supper. It served me right for being so greedy. Instead I had a pack of Ramen noodles with crackers, a bagel with honey and peanut butter, a granola bar topped off with a cup of that good chamomile tea I had bought in Rexford.

While we were eating we started having issues with mice. They were hanging around our tents looking for crumbs. No sooner would we chase one away then another one was snooping around. There seemed to be several families of them in the area. Mervin clapped his hands at one to shoo it away. We had to make sure our food was out of their reach and keep our tent zippers tightly closed or we might have unwelcome visitors in the night.

As usual we put our food in stuff sacks and pulled them up in a tree branch with ropes out of mice or bears reach. At dusk an owl hooted in the distance. I hoped he might take care of some of the mice.

As darkness crept over the land, the air cooled down fast, the sky was cloudless and I thought to myself, "This would be a good night for stargazing if I'm not too lazy to get out of my sleeping bag."

At 10:25 P.M. I entered in my journal that it is now time for my horizontal position.

Saturday, July 25, at 3:10 A.M. I entered in my journal that I had just come back from stargazing. I was again awed and was glad I took the opportunity and made the effort to get up and go outside of my tent to stargaze.

There was no moon, the air was crisp and cool, and the sky was cloudless. I could see the cloudy film of the Milky Way with its countless stars and the Big Dipper. The Big Dipper looked the same as at home. I thought of how no matter where we are or what life throws at us, God is the same yesterday, today, and tomorrow. I saw shooting stars, stars right down to the horizon, and stars that looked like they were twinkling. It was a spectacular, awesome experience. I thought of the Jack Rich quote, "When all is said and done it recharges the part that cannot be seen." Scenes like this made all the hard hiking, the heavy Klutz, the blisters and the aching muscles seem like minor inconveniences. I went back in my tent and snuggled in my sleeping bag, grateful for the privilege to experience the awe-inspiring wilderness at its best.

That morning when I got up it was forty-five degrees, not as chilly as the previous mornings. I went fishing before breakfast, hoping to have fresh fish with my oatmeal. The fish weren't biting so I had oatmeal with Swiss Miss, cheese sticks and Dove candy.

Then Mervin came proudly back from fishing with three fish. I thought, "Now that's not fair." I decided to try again because I was still a little hungry. After much casting I finally landed an eleven-inch trout, cleaned and cooked it right away for lunch.

At 11:55, I entered in my journal that I am ready to hit the trail. The Klutz was getting a break. According to my calculations we only had two or three miles to Big Salmon Lake where we intended to camp for the night. According to the map there wasn't a lot of climbing to do either.

We didn't do any fishing until we got to Big Salmon Lake.

Somehow I had misjudged my mileage, for when we got to Big Salmon Lake it was at least six miles of hiking and to get to the lake we went up a ways yet. So much for the easy day for Ole Klutz.

*Dead bull trout choked on half-swallowed fish on the banks of Big Salmon Lake. Note the tail of half-swallowed fish sticking out of the bull trout's mouth.*

We came to the lake at 3:30. A strong wind was blowing across the lake right at our campsite. Big Salmon Lake is the largest lake in the Bob Marshall Wilderness complex and is four miles long and half a mile wide, 4300 feet above sea level. With high mountains rising above the lake on each side, it is like a huge, natural wind tunnel. Any wind that blows across the lake gets funneled towards the outlet where we intended to camp.

We set our packs down and munched on our trail snacks while we pondered the wisdom of setting up our tents in the wind.

We didn't come to a definite decision right away. I decided to at least see if the fish are biting. I took my spinning rod with a spoon bait because I figured with the stiff wind it would be tough to cast against the wind into the lake with a fly. I cast a few times and no bites. I went around to the north side of the lake where I thought it might not be as windy and maybe there would be a campsite there away from the wind. The fish weren't biting there either and I didn't find any decent tentsites. I almost lost my spoon bait on snags so I gave it up.

When I got back to where we had dropped our packs Elam decided to walk a little farther around the north trail and see if he couldn't find a better site.

"I might as well take my Saturday night bath while we wait," I thought. I went down the stream that flowed out of the lake until I found a pool of clear water. The water was blitzing cold, but I felt like a new man when I was done. Nothing like a bath in a cold mountain stream to refresh a body and cool blistered feet. My feet were still causing me grief and every night I had to doctor them with salve. In the morning I covered the blisters with duct tape to prevent more chafing.

Elam didn't find anything better so we went back down to the Flathead River away from the wind. Our campsite was just a little upstream from where Big Salmon Creek flowed into the Flathead River. It was a nice sandy area about twenty feet down a steep bank from trail number 263.

The fishing was good, and we each had our limit of three fish that day. I cooked them in our little pan with olive oil, added a little salt, and had them with a bagel, peanut butter and honey. Fresh trout in the wilderness cannot be beat. I topped it off with a steaming cup of tea with honey, and at 10:25 P.M. I entered in my journal that I am ready to retire for the night.

Sunday morning, July 26, I slept in until 8:00. I had a nice sandy, flat spot for my tentsite with no rocks or roots to disturb my slumber. It rained that night, but no more than a couple tenths. The rain woke me, but it didn't last long and I was soon asleep again. Raindrops on a tent that stays dry inside can be very soothing in the wilderness as long as it doesn't become very windy or stormy. There was some thunder but nothing real close.

Since it was Sunday, I took a break from fishing. For breakfast I had the last of my granola cereal, string cheese, pistachio nuts, and a cup of Swiss Miss with honey. While we were eating breakfast, Mervin and I had a discussion about the world's problems. The topic was fashions, and we got into it pretty deep. Nothing like the wilderness on a Sunday morning to stimulate a lively discussion.

*Twenty-six inch bull trout that Elam caught.*

It was warmer that morning, fifty degrees, mostly cloudy with patches of sunshine.

At 12:30 I packed up and left camp (before the others were quite ready) for a Sunday afternoon stroll of two or three miles to the next campsite at Little Salmon Park.

I leisurely hiked along for about a mile until I came to a nice shaded area beside a creek where I spent a couple hours.

It was like an oasis. A lot of the areas that we hiked through were burned, and it could get very hot. Here the fires had somehow missed a small patch where the trees were big and green.

I dropped the Klutz, sat down, and leaned on the Klutz for a Sunday afternoon nap. I dozed for a while, read out of the small pocket Testament that I had packed, and watched the birds, squirrels, and chipmunks scamper around. I saw woodpeckers, chickadees, juncos and lots of other small birds I couldn't name. It was so peaceful and quiet I could have stayed there all day.

Soon Mervin and Elam came along and we had a snack.

Elam didn't stay long and left for the next campsite. He left his fishing rods lay that he had been carrying and had them setting against a tree. Mervin and I decided we might as well take them along so he wouldn't have to come back for them.

Before we got started we had another discussion about the world's problems. This time we discussed how, often, when people aren't satisfied with the church they are in and leave for a "better" church, they soon are dissatisfied and try another church. This can go on and on until after a few years it looks almost as if they don't belong to a church. We got into it pretty deep until the next thing we knew Elam was back for his poles about an hour later. He had hiked about a mile and a half before he missed them. Not knowing if we would notice them, much less bring them along, he hiked all the way back to get them. The extra three miles he hiked to get the rods didn't seem to hurt him a bit.

The two or three mile stroll to Little Salmon Park stretched out to 4.2 miles. Little Salmon Park was a nice flat area by the river where we could tell that the river got very wide during flooding. To get to the river we had to cross a couple hundred feet of sand and rocks. There were piles of tangled trees and branches to go around, too.

We set up camp under live pines. For supper, I had a bagel with honey and peanut butter, potatoes, topped off with a cup of tea. The potatoes were dried powder, and mixed with hot water it was a tasty meal.

At 9:15 I entered in my journal that it's time to hit the sack. The leisurely day had given my feet a break, and the blisters were healing, although I still kept them covered with duct tape.

Monday, July 27, I got up at 6:30 and went fishing. It was forty-five degrees, cloudy and chilly. I couldn't get a single fish to bite.

I was going from one fishing hole to the next over a flat area of sand and rocks when I came across a bird that went crazy when it saw me. It looked like an eastern quail but a little bigger. It squawked, flapped its wings and looked like it was hurt, trying to get my attention. It acted a lot like the killdeer does when they have a nest close by.

Sure enough, when I searched away from the area where the bird was acting injured I found two little birds among the stones. They were very well camouflaged, and if the mother bird wouldn't have gotten my attention I could easily have stepped on them without seeing them. Another wonder of nature. This time it was a little thing but very impressive.

I gave up trying to catch fish that morning. I settled with oatmeal for breakfast, cooked on my little stove. While I was waiting for the oatmeal to cool I made another entry in my journal.

It rained off and on all day and for the first time I had use for my rain gear. It didn't rain hard at all, just light rain now and then with low-hanging heavy clouds. Just enough to keep everything wet and cool that wasn't covered.

I left camp around 9:30. About a mile on the trail, the trail drifted away from the river on the side of the ridge and I saw where the river made a sharp turn about half a mile away. "Now, that would possibly be an excellent fishing hole," I thought.

Soon I came to a side trail that looked like it might lead down to the river. Elam and Mervin were nowhere near so I decided to take it. It was a good half mile to the river, and the side trail led me right to the river at a beautiful campsite. The bend in the river that I wanted to fish was another quarter mile downriver from the campsite.

I dropped the Klutz, grabbed my fishing gear and bear spray, and went through the thick bushes, hoping I wouldn't come across any bears on the way.

The rain kept falling lightly but steadily. Across the river on the next ridge a long pack train was following another trail heading south. I watched them through my binoculars marveling at the simplicity of the wilderness in this modern day and age. It gave me a new appreciation for the laws and effort to keep the wilderness wild and pristine.

I got to the hole I was after and was pleased to see how deep it was. The river made a sharp turn with big boulders sticking out of the water and deep pools around the rocks.

I took my spinning rod and tied on a large white streamer. I figured I'd try for bull trout right away. I cast into one of the pools and watched the streamer float along. Suddenly I felt a jerk in the line, enough that I knew this was no ordinary fish. I quickly tightened my rod but then it let loose. I reeled it in and cast again, but this time my hook got caught on one of the rocks. I jerked, pulled and carried on, but the hook held fast. I didn't have to worry so much about breaking my rod because I was using a spinning reel, but I didn't much like the idea of losing a three dollar streamer.

I studied the situation and decided if I could get on the big flat rock that jutted out of the water about ten feet across, I could probably loosen my hook. But to get there I had to cross swift water that was well over knee deep. I had several options to choose from: I could jerk and tug on my line and very likely break it, wade across and get my shoes and pants wet, or, take my pants and shoes off.

I chose to take my pants and shoes off.

I unlaced my shoes, pulled them off, slipped my socks off, peeled off my rainpants and pants, covered everything the best I could with my rainpants (it was still raining) and stood there barefooted in my underwear and raincoat feeling rather foolish. But I didn't care. This was the wilderness where you do things you wouldn't do anywhere else. Besides, there was nobody around to see me and I was having fun.

I sorely wished for my watershoes, but I had left those in the Klutz. Carefully I stepped into the water on the slippery rocks. The water was cold and came well over my knees, but it felt good to my blistered feet.

I worked my way across safely until I came to the flat rock. From the rock I easily loosened the hook.

From the position I was in I could cast a lot better into the pool where the big fish had struck. I cast a few times but had no more bites so I worked my way back to the river bank.

Back on the river bank I couldn't forget that fish. I had more streamers of various colors in my bait box so I tied a black one on with shiny flecks on it.

But from the shore I couldn't cast very well to the pool I wanted to. Oh well, now that I had wet legs and was dressed to be in the water—or rather undressed—I thought I might as well go out to the flat rock again.

I waded back, climbed onto the rock, cast into the deep pool and bam, another great tug on my rod. Again the big trout spit out the streamer before it hooked. Now I was really excited! I cast a few more times with no bites. I waded back to the shore and tied on a green streamer.

Four or five times I tied on a different color streamer, waded out to the flat rock, cast into the pool and the fish would strike but spit it out before the hook caught. I lost all track of time and finally he quit striking altogether. I was certain it had been a bull trout. Several times I caught a glimpse of him through the clear water and I could tell it was more than just a mere minnow. He would hide under a ledge where I couldn't see him and the water was rushing along, which made it even harder to see the fish.

Finally I gave up on this particular fish. I waded back to the shore where I had left my pants and shoes. By this time it had quit raining but there was still heavy cloud cover with an occasional drop of rain.

I didn't bother waiting until I was dry to pull my pants and socks on. When I was fully dressed again I felt a little more normal. I decided to try and catch a smaller trout for lunch. I took my fly rod and went below the deep pool where I caught a ten-inch cutthroat.

I was hungry so I gathered my gear and the fish and went back through the thick bushes to where I had left the Klutz. When I dropped the Klutz I had no intention of staying so long at the fishing hole. I hoped no bears had found the Klutz because I knew we were in bear country. I hated to think what a bear could do to a pack. As I went through the thick brush I kept my bear spray in hand; I felt it would be pretty easy to sneak on a bear unawares. The Klutz was still there, undisturbed and covered with his own waterproof cover. It was like seeing a good friend again, and I felt a kinship with him even if he made me want to complain at times.

How much like a good friend the Klutz was. True friends will sometimes do and say things that make us mad and hurt us, but in friendships that last we are always glad to see them again even if they have hurt us in the past.

I took my little stove and pan and cooked the fish in olive oil on the spot. It was delicious. A couple handfuls of trail nuts and a few pieces of Dove candy recharged me, ready to hit the trail again.

All this had taken a great deal of time, and when I checked my watch as I hit the trail I was shocked to see that it was 2:30 already. I had a four or five mile hike to where we had planned to camp that night.

It was still cool, cloudy, and wet with an occasional shower. I kept my raingear on even if it wasn't raining because the wet bushes along the trail would soon soak me without raingear.

With the cool rain on the trail, my feet didn't bother me as much. I decided the socks I was wearing are for spring and fall weather, not for the hot summer. But I couldn't very well go to a store and buy others, and doing without would be even worse. I had to learn to deal with it.

# Chapter Five: Fishing the South Fork of the Flathead

A few miles farther I came to the Black Bear forest service cabin that had smoke coming from the chimney. There was no sign of Elam or Mervin so I went and knocked on the door. I was greeted by a pretty young lady who invited me inside.

There were three ladies there for the night. Two of them were river rangers who went along in boats, checked campsites along the river for trash, and cleaned up after sloppy campers.

The other lady was on a weeds crew. The weeds crew went along the trails spraying noxious or non-native weeds.

They were friendly, offered me a chair and Gatorade, which I gratefully accepted. The warmth from the fire felt good, and after a week on the trail with men and their competitive spirit, the feminine companionship was nice.

I visited with them for a while. The lady on the weeds crew was from Pottsville, PA, only an hour's drive from my place. She had even done some winter hiking in the Adirondack Mountains in New York. It was amazing meeting someone in the Bob Marshall Wilderness who was from that close to home.

They hadn't seen anything of Elam or Mervin. I figured they probably were long past there.

I thanked them for the Gatorade and went to the packbridge that the ladies had directed me to. They said there were campsites across the river, but when I came to the sites there was no sign of Mervin or Elam. I searched around and found another campsite but nobody was there. As I was debating if I want to hike a little farther I decided to whistle. I blew a long, hard whistle. To my surprise, a whistle answered. It was Mervin. They had found a beautiful campsite along the river a few hundred yards from the packbridge on the opposite side of the river. The forest was thick in that area, and the river made a sharp bend so I couldn't see them from where I was. I was glad that thanks to our whistles I wouldn't have to spend the night alone.

It was 6:30 when I found the other guys. This was our last campsite beside the South fork of the Flathead. It looked like a good spot to catch fish, but the fish weren't biting well that night. I did catch one for supper after much casting.

Mervin was determined to catch a fish for supper that night. He fished until past 9:00 when finally, after a couple hours he caught a nice eleven-inch trout. One thing I learned about flyfishing in the wilderness; the river may be filled with fish but if they don't feel like biting they will not.

It had been a cooler day with rain on and off with a high around sixty degrees. The cool weather helped my feet. They didn't get as hot on the wet trail.

At 9:45 I crawled in my tent and made another entry in my journal. We had hiked only five miles that day.

Tuesday morning, July 28, dawned chilly and cloudy with the temperature at forty-five degrees. It had rained that night but didn't amount to much. I got up at 6:30 and went fishing but caught nothing. I settled for oatmeal, Swiss Miss and honey with my protein shake for breakfast.

When I was done eating Mervin came to camp with three fish. I thought I was satisfied, but I found that I am always hungry for fresh trout even after a meal. I tried again, and this time I caught one. I cooked and ate it right away and was ready to leave camp by 8:30.

Now we were leaving the South Fork of the Flathead River and heading to the high county where we would get into some serious hiking. I had mixed feelings about leaving the beautiful Flathead. For four days we had fished and camped at the river. But it was time to get to the next phase of our hike, and the route we were taking would bring us across the Continental Divide to the east side of the wilderness.

I was beginning to understand what Mr. Rich had meant when he said the wilderness recharges the part that cannot be seen. The river had touched me deep in my heart in different ways that I cannot explain. I felt like I was leaving a little piece of my heart at the river waiting to be picked up later.

# Chapter Six:
# Hiking the High Country

I hoisted the Klutz onto my back, left camp, and as we crossed the pack-bridge to the other side I took a last look at the river that had done so much for me. Resolutely I turned away, ready for the next challenge.

We took trail number 80 about a mile and a half, then made a left on Helen Creek trail number 100.

Right at the intersection where a couple trails came together, I came upon a beautiful mule deer buck about twenty yards away. He had a wide, tall rack that still had velvet, with a total of nine points. He was coming directly toward me on the trail. I stopped and stared at him awhile until he decided he doesn't like me after all. He veered off the trail into the thick woods to let me pass. It seemed like the mule deer were not nearly as spooky as whitetails in the wilderness.

At the Helen Creek trail we started going up. The Flathead River elevation was 4500 feet, while the top of Pagoda Mountain where we were headed was 8041 feet.

For ten miles we went up, on and on and on.

A couple of miles up we came to a raspberry patch where we feasted on raspberries. Later there were huckleberries to feast on. And the trail kept going up.

At one spot the trail crossed the north fork of Helen Creek where we could get fresh water. We didn't fill our water bottles there because according to our maps the creek was on up. Elam and I were hiking with each other then, with Mervin behind us. Soon we discovered we couldn't see or hear the creek anymore. There was a steep ravine to our right down to what looked like a dry creek bed. We set our packs down and discussed the situation.

*Huckleberries*

We decided that, although our maps indicated a creek, apparently it had dried up. After all, it was pretty dry. We took our filters and water bottles back to where the trail had crossed the creek. It was about a quarter mile to the creek. As we came down we heard Mervin humming to himself while he was filling his bottles. He couldn't see us because there were thick bushes along the creek between him and us.

It was too much for Elam. He sneaked down the trail behind the bushes until he was about ten feet from Mervin. Mervin was leisurely filtering water into his bottle when Elam, with a terrible roar, jumped out from the bushes right at him. Mervin let out a frightened squeak and looked like he was ready to drop his water bottles and run. But instantly he saw who it was and his fear turned into disgust. He laughed along with us and was a good sport about it. We all knew that each of us would have our turn.

We filled up with water and went back to our packs. The elevation there was 5000 feet, and we had a long hike ahead of us.

A little farther on we discovered that Helen Creek was visible again to our right. Apparently it had flowed underground awhile. Oh well, we were now carrying enough of water for the rest of the day so we kept plodding on.

Up and up we went. At 6500 feet I felt like we came a long way already. We were above some of the smaller peaks but when I checked my map I saw we were only a little more than halfway to the top. So we plodded on.

At 7500 feet the trees thinned out and we were treated to incredible views. The trail hugged the side of the mountain with steep shale going down on the right and steep cliffs and shale going up on our left. We saw sign of bighorn sheep or mountain goats, we didn't know which. So far we hadn't seen any. Another sign that we were in high country.

Finally, nine miles up from the Flathead River we came to where the Helen Creek trail number 100 met with the Pagoda Mountain trail number 220. It was another mile, and 500 feet up, to the top of Pagoda Mountain.

We took a short break, grabbed some snacks from our packs, left our packs by the trail and headed for the top. Without our packs the going was a lot easier and I'm sure the Klutz was glad for the break.

At 8041 feet we finally made it to the top, ten miles from the Flathead River and 3500 feet higher. All the pain and toil of plodding up the trail fell away in those first moments on the top.

The views were incredible. All we could see was wilderness in every direction. Below us the South Fork of the Flathead snaked through the valley. To the west, south, and north there was peak after peak stretching into the distance as far as we could see. To the east was the Continental Divide, where the mountains rose more gradually and dropped sharply down on the other side. Some of the neighboring peaks that were higher than Pagoda Peak still had snow on them. Seeing peaks that were almost a thousand feet higher made me feel small. I thought of all these tall peaks, how God created them and that He is bigger than any mountain that we can and cannot see. That would include any mountain or obstacle in our minds too.

I felt the (now becoming familiar) feeling of being touched in places that cannot be seen. The grandeur, the vastness, the beauty, the wildness of being in the very heart of the wilderness—with not as much as a cabin or road in sight—cannot be expressed by mere words.

I like to think that heaven will be that way. The Bible teaches us that man

*Views from the trail leading to the top of Pagoda Mountain.*

*View to the south from the top of Pagoda Mountain
with Turtlehead Mountain in the foreground.*

*Looking east down into the White River drainage from Pagoda Peak.*

*Peaks with snowfields in the background southwest from Pagoda Peak.*
*Note the trail hugging the side of the mountain on the right.*

*Looking west from Pagoda Peak. Snowfields on the Mission Mountains in the background, Big Salmon Lake between the mountains with the South Fork of the Flathead River flowing in the valley below us.*

has not seen, or heard, nor entered into his heart what God has prepared for those who love him. We cannot imagine or grasp how it will be until we are there. That is how the wilderness is. I can try and describe the vastness and the beauty of it, but for someone to truly grasp it they must experience it. But the wilderness is not heaven. There is pain, hunger, and thirst in the wilderness, while in heaven there is only peace, love, and joy.

We were up so high it almost made me giddy to look down over the cliffs and valleys below. It was chilly up there, and a sweater felt good as we munched on our snacks.

Finally it was time to leave. We still had some miles to hike to the White

River at the next campsite. It didn't take long to hike the mile down to the main trail where we had left our packs. They were where we had left them so we hoisted them to our backs and began the descent down the other side. Down, down we went.

On the way down we got into a discussion of how these mountains were formed. One theory was that during the Great Flood the water came from the bottom up and the top down. This could have pushed the earth up and crested these mountains and cliffs. The area in the Continental Divide has a sort of pattern. The mountains slope more gradually to the west while in the east side they drop abruptly down, thousands of feet.

The discussion and theories ended when Elam said, "God does not just do things because he can. He usually designs things so they work."

I thought he made an excellent point. As wild and vast as the wilderness is, there is still a harmony in it. And yet, God has created man to be stewards of all he has created. A noble and high calling that we need to take seriously.

And still we kept going down. We descended about 2000 feet in five miles when we came to the White River. It was not much more than a stream, with only small fish in it. We crossed the river and a marshy spot, then came to a beautiful place called Brushy Park. There was a campsite there with excellent tentsites and a fire ring. We immediately decided to camp there. At 6000 feet we were 1500 feet higher than at the South Fork of the Flathead River. We had hiked sixteen miles that day. Wearily we dropped our packs, grateful for the nice campsite.

The Klutz had held up as well as could be expected. I didn't hear him creak as much as I felt like creaking. We were now halfway through our hike, and I wondered how the next half would be like. One thing, the Klutz wasn't as heavy anymore, something I looked forward to in the next half of our hike.

We set up camp and decided tonight we are going to have a fire. There was a fire ring there, the grass and trees around were green, so we figured it would be safe. We hadn't seen a single other person all day since we hit the Helen Creek trail.

We soon had a cheerful blaze going. For the first time we cooked our meal on an open fire. We didn't think it was worth trying to catch fish because the fish we had seen were tiny in the White River. The South Fork of the Flathead had spoiled us with its plentiful cutthroat, and besides, we were ready to retire for the night.

# Chapter Six: Hiking the High Country

After a good meal I brewed a cup of tea before bedtime. It was a beautiful evening. The sky was clear, the air crisp, and it was wonderful to sit on a log around the fire, drinking tea, thinking back over the day, and enjoying the clear mountain air.

The mule deer were claiming the spot too. They came so close that we had to chase them away. I hoped they wouldn't disturb us in the night.

As dusk settled in, I laid my used teabag on the log, helped put out the fire, and wearily crawled into my tent to give my body much-needed rest.

My blisters were acting up again after hiking sixteen miles that day. My duct tape was about gone so I borrowed some from Elam. He had plenty. I figured if I go hiking again I would take more along and if I felt any hotspots on my feet I would stop and address them immediately. But then, I hadn't counted on my flyrod breaking, which used up a great deal of the precious tape. The thick wool socks I was wearing hadn't helped any either. But how could I expect everything to be perfect? This was the wilderness, where we have to make do with what we had.

Wednesday, July 29, I got up feeling like a new man. I had heard the mule deer sniffing around our tents a time or two, but they hadn't disturbed me much. A good night's sleep in the cool mountain air had done wonders. The morning dawned, crisp, clear and cold, with temperatures in the upper thirties.

The mule deer were gone and so was the teabag I had set on the log. I hoped they enjoyed the little treat.

We had breakfast, wrapped up camp, and took trail number 112 to Larch Hill Pass that would take us across the Continental Divide to the Chinese Wall. With all the miles we hiked the day before we slept longer that morning and had a late start. I hadn't gotten up until 8:30.

Soon after we left camp we met a party of about twenty people at a burned section of the wilderness. We nodded good-morning to them and went on our way. For a whole day we hadn't seen a single soul but ourselves. It was a reminder that the wilderness is to be shared.

It was five miles to the top of Larch Hill Pass, elevation 7800 feet. On the 1800 foot climb we again feasted on wild huckleberries. They only grew on the south and west slopes. We were there in peak season and we feasted on huckleberries like I never did before.

The first guy to come to a patch would drop his pack and stuff ripe huckleberries in his mouth. The next guy to come along would help himself awhile, then move on, hoping to come upon a patch for himself. We hiked on up to Larch Hill Pass, eating huckleberries until we satisfied ourselves. It seemed like they grew the best between 6500 and 7000 feet. I don't know what the calories are per ounce in huckleberries. Probably not even close to one hundred calories per ounce, but very likely they made the calories in the food we carried go farther. As good as they were, I'm sure they were good for something.

The sun shone bright and warm as we trudged on up to the top of Larch Hill Pass. We were still on trail number 112 and when we got to the top we were just above the tree line.

We had a choice to take trail number 175 across the pass down to the Chinese Wall where we wanted to camp, which was about a mile, or take trail number 739 around by My Lake, which was over four miles. Since it was early afternoon and trail number 739 looked to be more scenic and less traveled, we chose that route.

The trail hugged the side of the ridge just wide enough to walk single file. On our right the ridge rose steeply another couple hundred feet while to our left it dropped sharply down hundreds of feet into a trail-less valley. We took a short break for snacks at a spot where we could sit on some rocks and enjoy the view across the valley.

It was a whistle clear day. To the north we could see the craggy peaks of Glacier Park, probably fifty miles away. It was mind boggling how far we could see and nothing but total wilderness. There was not a single road, house or any kind of manmade structure in sight, anywhere. The only sign that man had ever been in the area was the narrow trail we were on.

About a mile farther on I came to a grassy spot where I took another break to write in my journal at 3:00. The wildflowers were gorgeous there. Late July is peak season for flowers in the high country. There were many different colors in white, red, blue, orange, yellow, and purple in different hues that all blended together to create a delightful smorgasbord for my eyes. I could lift up my eyes to see huge mountains and vast distances, or, when I lowered my eyes there were beautiful flowers, trees and green grass to look at. I hardly knew which way to look, or when to stop looking and move on to the next view. This was true wilderness paradise.

From where I was sitting I could see what they call the Chinese Wall. The Chinese Wall is a sheer cliff that stretches for twelve miles right on the

# Chapter Six: Hiking the High Country

Continental Divide. The cliffs on the Wall have a sheer drop of a thousand feet or more at some places. This is the spot where, as I will quote, "When a raindrop falls on the divide and splits, one half merrily flows west to the Pacific, while the other half merrily rolls to the east into the Atlantic."

But it wasn't all gravy. When you have plodded up a mountain for a thousand feet, stop and take a break from the hard climbing and you realize that you have two thousand more feet to go in five miles, it can make you wonder, "Why am I doing this," or "This is crazy." But once you reach the top you see why. When you reach the spot where you realize that you can't go any higher, all the pain and toil of climbing melts away and goes crashing down the mountain.

Life is like that. We come to a place in life where after much labor and toil, all seems well and good. But we never stay in the same place long. God allows thing to happen that are beyond our control, or, from our own mistakes, that take us down in a valley where we wonder if God really cares. But if we keep going, trust and believe in God, He will bring good out of any situation in ways we never dreamed of.

Going down from Larch Hill Pass we crossed the Continental Divide and were now on the east side of the Bob Marshall Wilderness Complex. Just before My Lake we connected to the Continental Divide Trail, (CDT). The CDT Trail stretches from Canada to Mexico along the Continental Divide for over 2000 miles. We could tell it was more heavily traveled then the trail on Larch Hill Pass had been.

At My Lake someone had set up a camp with a large tent. My Lake was just a small lake. We only stopped to fill our water bottles and have a snack before we moved on. Our goal was to camp somewhere along the Chinese Wall.

Now that we were east of the divide all the springs and streams flowed east and south toward home. Somehow (even though we had just crossed the divide) it felt like we were much closer to home. Now it felt like we were on the homestretch. The CDT was trail number 175 in that area.

We found a beautiful campsite at the foot of the Chinese Wall where the cliffs towered above us at least a thousand feet. There were a few small springs nearby where we had plenty of fresh water.

*At the foot of the Chinese Wall close to where we camped.*

*The Chinese wall from the CDT trail.*

*View to the east from the Chinese Wall.*

*Looking back toward Larch Hill Pass from the Chinese Wall. The ledge on the wall is where the mountain goats were. The CDT trail is in the foreground.*

As we were searching for a campsite I thought I saw movement at the very top of the wall. Quickly I grabbed my binoculars to get a closer look. Way up high, silhouetted against the setting sun, was a flock of mountain goats walking along the rim of the wall. At first I thought there was only one or two, but when we were setting up camp we discovered it was a flock of about fifteen to twenty of them.

They came out on a ledge about five hundred feet up, directly above our campsite. The ledge had grassy areas where they grazed as they went. There was a bunch of little ones in the flock that were still nursing. Without binoculars they weren't much more than specks.

I almost couldn't stop watching them and when one of the kids started nursing I suddenly had an intense craving for a glass of ice cold milk. I thought, "Mervin would be just the guy to go up there and milk one of them." I dared him to do it, but no, he vehemently declared he wouldn't, not even for a thousand dollars. Fresh goat milk would have been wonderful before bedtime, but this was a hiking trip and luxuries like that were not likely.

Fearlessly, the goats walked along the ledge, often at the very edge of the sheer cliffs that dropped down five hundred feet to the bottom where our camp was. Occasionally they would knock down loose rocks that came tumbling down with a clatter. There was a heap of loose rocks at the bottom of the cliff. Our camp was far enough away that we weren't in any danger from falling rocks that the goats knocked down. I almost became giddy watching them at the very edges of the cliff.

The high cliffs and the steep ledge gave the goats all the protection they needed from predators. No bear, wolf, or mountain lion would dare cross that ledge to get to them. And no human would dare cross that ledge to milk them either. The only way to get them would be with a high powered rifle. We were in the Sun River Game Preserve where no hunting is allowed so they were safe from that, too. We contented ourselves with watching them.

There were pika to watch, too. Pika are interesting creatures. They look almost like a rat, but are in the rabbit family, with long ears and no visible tails. They make their homes on rocks by cliffs where they gather bunches of grass and lay it on the rocks to dry for food in the winter. Literally, they make hay like we do for our livestock. I had never even heard of pika before, but Elam, with his encyclopedic knowledge seemed to know all about them.

I watched one through my binoculars gather a great mouthful of grass, then go scampering under a rock with it. It must have been a scrumptious supper. How nice that would be to live on grass and we wouldn't have to carry our heavy packs. All we would need to do when we hike is first find a grassy area with water, pitch our tents, and have a feast.

Living in the wilderness with all the wild animals made me think of how God provides food for animals both great and small. We could see how the fish survived on bugs, the goats, deer, elk, and pika on grass, and the wolves, bears and mountain lions, on other animals. It drove home the fact that there always have to be more vegetarian animals than meat-eaters or the meat-eaters wouldn't survive. God has designed nature to take care of itself and there is an abundance for everyone and everything.

We hiked 9.3 miles that day. At 8:55 P.M. the setting sun was still shining against the mountains in the distance, turning the dull gray rock into a beautiful, reddish brown color. Because of the high cliffs we hadn't seen the sun since 6:30.

That night I was again awakened by a mule deer sniffing around outside my tent. I was amazed that they aren't more wild.

I crawled out of my tent and was treated to an awe-inspiring sight of the full moon shining down in the valley below us. It was a beautiful night. With the moon about full the stargazing wasn't as good, but the light from the moon created another kind of breathtaking beauty.

The moon lit the valley before us with soft tranquil light, while the cliffs of the Chinese Wall towered darkly above us to the west. Then there was the incredible silence. There is something about the vast silence in the wilderness that did things to my heart that can't be explained.

I stood there for a while, drinking in the scene, letting the beauty, the silence and the wildness of it all soak into the core of my being. I thought of the mountain goats high up on the ledge above us safe from predators. In the semi darkness they couldn't be seen. Only God knows the thoughts I thought. I thought thoughts that cannot be expressed with mere words. It felt as if the wilderness was trying to tell me something that I couldn't quite grasp. Or maybe it was God's way of speaking to me. I wished I could take this scene along home and share it with my loved ones.

I crawled back into my tent and snuggled into my sleeping bag, grateful for the opportunity to see the wilderness in the moonlight.

The next morning, Thursday, July 30, the eleventh day of our hike, I awoke to the warm rays of the sun shining against my tent. It had been a chilly night, with temperatures hovering around forty degrees or less.

The blisters on my feet were feeling better so I left the duct tape on from the day before. I knew that keeping the hot spots on my feet covered with duct tape kept them from heating up as much. Duct tape is like a second skin and prevents chafing.

For breakfast I had oatmeal with wild garlic and Swiss Miss, a stick of string cheese, and my protein shake.

High above us on the ledge the mountain goats were soaking up the early morning sunshine. They looked like specks without binoculars, and we could hardly see them unless they moved.

Around 8:00 they started moving back to where we first saw them the night before. Again they walked fearlessly on the ledge and the edge of the precipices, hundreds of feet high. I was lying on my back with my head resting on the Klutz watching them through my binoculars. I could hardly stop watching them while the kids nursed, and the big billies sauntered along, knocking down loose stones that occasionally came tumbling down the cliffs. I wondered if the pika at the bottom never got hit by the rocks that the goats knocked down. They wouldn't stand a chance if one of the rocks would hit them. But life is not without risks. The chance of us being involved in a train wreck on our way home was probably a lot higher than the pika being hit by falling rock that the mountain goats knocked down.

At last it was time to move on. I put down my binoculars and finished packing up camp. I stepped over the Klutz and my foot clumsily caught on my borrowed fly rod that was sticking out of the top. With a sickening snap the six inches that stuck out because of the splint broke off. Quickly I bent down and examined the broken rod. With chagrin I realized the rod was broken beyond repair. I berated myself for being so careless and not watching my step more. But the damage was done and I would have to deal with it.

At one of the forest service cabins along the Flathead one of the rangers had said spoon bait on a spinning rod can work well for trout. I had a single spoon with my tackle so I figured I'd try that at the next fishing hole. Once again it struck me how we were very much on our own and would have to do with what we had. Only in an extreme emergency would we use our satellite phone for outside help.

As we were packing up camp, one of the two hikers who had been camped about half a mile in the direction we came from, came into our camp and asked us if we had seen one of his hiking poles. He said he had placed them by their camp leaning against a log. Now this morning one was missing. He looked at Elam as he spoke. We had passed them at their campsite the evening before and Elam had walked back to their site to ask if they knew if campfires are allowed this side of the divide. They hadn't known for sure so we hadn't built a fire.

Now this man was insinuating that Elam might have taken one of his walking sticks. This was almost too much for Elam. He couldn't believe someone would accuse him of taking someone else's walking stick in the wilderness.

But he exercised complete self-control and assured the man he hadn't seen his walking stick. That didn't completely satisfy him for he said, "I know I left them leaning against the log and now this morning one is gone."

"Maybe the mule deer got it." I suggested. "This is the stick I use." I showed him the wooden pine stick I carried. This didn't seem to make him very happy and he soon left camp. Obviously he still suspected us, for he couldn't wrap his mind around it that a walking stick would walk away by itself.

Elam almost didn't get over it that someone would accuse him of stealing a walking stick. It is mind-boggling that people are so suspicious of each other and trust no one. But this world is so full of sin and hurt and very likely this man had a deep hurt in his life where someone betrayed or rejected him whom he had trusted. Then when his walking stick was missing he quickly suspected Elam because he was the only person besides him and his partner who could have known that the sticks were there.

It was unnerving to us to have someone come into our camp like that and blame us for something we didn't do. Here we were in the wilderness away from civilization where all is supposed to be peace and solitude. But it doesn't matter where we go, as long as there are people there are problems.

Later we had a good laugh at the absurdity that Elam would go in somebody's camp and take only one walking stick. Then we tried to imagine this man hiking along with only one stick and checking each hiker that he met for his other stick. The image was so ridiculous as to be funny, now that we were over the shock of being accused for stealing. Very likely he found it after he searched around a little for it.

As we packed up and left camp the mountain goats were almost back to the place on the wall where we had first seen them the night before. I took one last look at them with my binoculars, hoisted the Klutz on my back, and followed the CDT trail along the wall.

The trail took us along the Chinese Wall for several miles and about a mile from the camp we entered a pristine area of the wilderness. There were signs along the trail stating that no camping was allowed for the next few miles. To our right the Chinese Wall towered above us with Cliff Mountain jutting up to 8566 feet behind the wall. On our left Moose Creek flowed away from the wall down through the valley that was covered with beautiful pine forests.

At Cliff Mountain we took a short side trail as far as we dared up the wall. The trail took us almost to the top of the wall but sheer cliffs a couple hundred feet higher prevented us from reaching the top. We sat there for a while enjoying the view. To the north the wall stretched a couple miles to Larch Hill Pass, while to the south the CDT trail followed the wall for about half a mile, then made a sharp left away from the wall while the wall stretched on into an extremely rough and trail-less section of unbroken wilderness. Up there on Cliff Mountain we could still see no sign of civilization.

We stayed on the CDT trail all day. There weren't as many hills to climb that day and the trail took us through beautiful pine forests where it wasn't as hot.

Once when I was walking along, the pine needle-covered forest floor looked so inviting I hiked about fifty yards from the trail, lay down and took a nap. It felt very good, alone there in the peaceful wilderness taking a break.

One thing the wilderness taught me; it is pointless to be in a hurry. Unless you are trying to see how many miles you can do in a day; hurrying from one place to the next makes no sense at all. Already we had changed from the route Elam had planned at the start. We had become so wrapped up in fishing the South Fork of the Flathead River that to reach the Mortimer Gulch trailhead by Tuesday afternoon we cut off a good fifty miles from our hike. Our plans had been to go around the north side of Silvertip Mountain and bushwhack to a lake called Christopher Lake that had no trails leading to it.

I think that was another one of the lessons the wilderness had for me, was to enjoy the beauty of now and not worry about reaching a certain point until the end of the day. How often in life do we reach so hard for our goals that we forget to enjoy today and to appreciate that this is the day that the Lord has made.

Later that afternoon we came to a nice campsite beside the west fork of the Sun River. We hiked a total of 14.6 miles that day and the camp looked inviting.

It had been a picture perfect day. The huge Montana sky was the clearest blue I had ever seen. The sun shone brightly, the trail had gone through shaded forests much of the way, and now we were at a campsite where we could have a fire. We had talked with someone who had said here in the east side of the divide—where it was more wet—we could have campfires. We wasted no time in building one and soon had hot coals to prepare our food.

As I dumped my food out of the Klutz I was shocked to see a stone roll out with my food. "However did that thing get into the Klutz!" I gasped to myself. Here I had been looking forward to a lighter pack, and now a stone had somehow, mysteriously found a way into my pack. No wonder I still had trouble with hot feet and blisters; carrying all that extra weight around sure didn't help anything.

"Okay, I won't say anything," I decided. "Whoever it was probably won't be able to keep it to himself."

I thought back over the day. I was sure I hadn't put it there by mistake. And I hadn't noticed any rocks growing on trees that could have fallen in the Klutz, although rocks were plentiful on the ground. I did remember that once when I was in front, one of the guys had given me a boost. The boost must have been a cover-up to put a stone in my pack. So much for what I thought to be a well meaning push. I'd have to figure out what I could do to play tricks, too. I was fairly certain it was Mervin, but Elam was right there too and would have seen it so he would be as much to blame as if he had done it. Making me walk five miles with all that extra weight was an atrocity that couldn't be taken lightly. So it goes; when a group of guys are together, tricks will be played.

Our camp was at the west fork of the Sun River. It was not much more than a stream and at home we would have called it a creek. Elam took his fly rod and cast a few times but didn't catch anything worth keeping. Mervin and I didn't bother.

After we had eaten our supper of trail food I washed myself in the ice cold river. I didn't stay in the water long, but it felt good to get at least some of the grime off of me. It also soothed the blisters on my feet.

Just before I crawled in my tent I noticed Mervin's tent behind mine and he was nowhere to be seen. Now I couldn't resist it. I grabbed a couple of rocks and put one where his head would be and one at his feet. I placed them under his tent hoping he wouldn't find them until he was ready to lie down in his warm sleeping bag.

At 8:40 I crawled into my tent, made an entry in my journal and rubbed petroleum jelly on my sore feet to try and soften them for the next day. I couldn't forget how I had to carry a stone that day and now my feet were sore.

The night passed uneventfully, and I hadn't heard a peep from Mervin. "Maybe I was blaming the wrong guy," I thought. "Or maybe he is playing the same game I am by not saying anything." At any rate, I figured time would reveal the truth.

The next morning, Friday, July 30 dawned clear and cold with the temperature at thirty-six degrees. We got up earlier because our plans were to hike to the top of Prairie Reef Mountain to a lookout at an elevation of 8858 feet.

I had breakfast, packed my gear, shouldered the Klutz, and by 8:00 I was on the trail. It was seven miles to the top of Prairie Reef and the early start in the cool morning air felt good.

We were still on the CDT trail. A short distance from camp I met a couple who were hiking the entire trail from Mexico to Canada. I stopped and talked with them. They talked about the high elevations of Colorado where the

*Prairie Reef trail just before the top.*
*The lookout cabin can be seen at the very top in the center of the picture.*

77

peaks stretch up to 12,000 feet. It made the 9,000 foot peaks of the Bob seem small by comparison. But the valleys of Colorado were at 8,000 to 9,000 feet so the climbs weren't that much different except for the altitude.

Then the lady said something that shed some light on the missing walking stick mystery. We were discussing how the mule deer could make such a pest out of themselves. She showed me her walking stick handle where a mule deer had chewed the foam grip for the salt from sweat. She said she has to be careful where she puts the stick at night or the mule deer will drag it around. It was one of those *aha* moments. When I had kiddingly remarked to the man with the missing stick that, "maybe the mule deer took it," I was probably 100 percent correct. How I wished I could tell the man what probably happened. But very likely he had found it by now and was ashamed for blaming us.

# Chapter Seven:
# Prairie Reef and Bear Lake

It was a nice two mile hike in the cool morning air to the Prairie Reef trailhead. At the trailhead there was a small wooden sign saying there was no water available from this point on. That meant we had to fill our water bladders and carry all our water for the whole day. The other guys hadn't caught up with me yet, so I filled all my water containers and set out for the 3400 foot climb.

It was a long, hard climb to the top. For five miles the trail went up and up and up some more. The Klutz wasn't as heavy anymore, but he still made me puff up that mountain. My knees were creaking, but I didn't feel any pain, so I didn't worry about it. The Klutz really didn't creak much anymore.

But still the trail went up. About two miles up I passed an older man and two women on the trail. I nodded a greeting and wondered to myself at seeing older folks like that on a trail like this. I had serious doubts that they would make it to the top.

But I kept plodding on. Soon I passed another group of about ten women who were taking a break along the trail. In this area we were high enough that we were starting to have great views.

One of the women asked how far it is to the top yet. I replied that I guessed we were about half way up.

And so I plodded on.

The trail kept becoming steeper with numerous switchbacks. As the trees thinned out I caught a glimpse of Elam a few hundred yards behind me. "I'm going to see if I can't beat him to the top this time," I thought.

So I pushed on. The air kept becoming thinner and frequent breaks were necessary.

Finally, the lookout at the top came into view. After the first glimpse of the lookout it was another half hour to an hour of hard climbing to get to it.

Around 12:00 I reached the lookout when I could go no higher. Wearily I dropped the Klutz, grateful that at last I could rest.

The fire ranger at the lookout was very friendly and showed me around. The lookout cabin had windows on all sides where the ranger could see all around.

As I stood there absorbing the spectacular views, once again, all the toil, pain, and sweat of climbing the mountain melted away.

*From the top of Prairie Reef looking down into the valley.*
*In the distance where there is a gap in the mountains,*
*the wheat fields of Montana can be faintly seen.*

*View to the north from Prairie Reef Mountain.*

*Bear Lake from the top of Prairie Reef.*

*Snowfield on the north side of Prairie Reef.*

To the north, west, and south there was nothing but total wilderness. Far off to the east through a gap in the mountains I caught a glimpse of the wheat fields of Montana. They were a great way off yet—probably fifty miles or a three-day hike—but to my farmer heart, the wheat fields were a beautiful sight. For twelve days I had seen nothing but wilderness, and seeing those wheat fields, even from this distance, pulled on my heartstrings.

The women I had passed soon reached the top but there was no sign of the older man and the two women. There were two men from Bozeman, Montana, on top when I came up and soon Elam and Mervin joined us, too. With the group of women, the two men from Bozeman, the ranger, and us, there was a good-sized group of people up there. The ranger – whose name was Rick – said he gets about 150 tourists up there in a summer. With the crowd that was there that day it would have been ten percent of the visitors in one day.

The long strenuous hike up to the top had about done us in. We rested, ate snacks, chatted with the ranger and Peter and Dan, while never tiring of the spectacular views. Peter and Dan were the men from Bozeman.

We were there chatting for a while when Elam asked Rick what that cloud was to the north towards Glacier Park. Elam wondered if it could be a forest fire. Rick took a closer look and got all excited. It was a forest fire and a huge one! Quickly he went into the cabin and radioed around trying to figure out if anyone else had seen it yet. He came out a few minutes later and said it was in Glacier Park.

It was a huge fire, and great billows of smoke went up into the sky. From where we stood it looked like a cloud on the horizon and the atmosphere was hazy in that direction. Otherwise the sky was cloudless which made for some awesome views. Seeing a forest fire of that size, even from this distance, was eerie. Just thinking how dry it was and the way our little fires that we made burned, made me realize the importance of being careful. But this fire was a great way off and nothing for us to be concerned about. Later we learned that the fire had shut down much of Glacier Park including the Going-to-the-Sun Road. I wondered how the people from Ohio whom we had met on the train had fared. They had planned to visit Glacier Park.

We stayed up there over three hours visiting with Rick, Peter, and Dan. Peter was a schoolteacher in Bozeman, and Dan was an economist. He studied the viability of using military products for civilian use; things like paint, electronics, gear, etc. They were interesting men and couldn't believe that we were so dumb as to haul our packs to the top of Prairie Reef because the trail ended at the top. When we told them how we planned to bushwhack to Bear Lake it made sense to them after all.

We sat among the rocks talking about a great variety of topics. Rick was an interesting character, too. He had served in the military, had travelled much of the world, and was a fantastic storyteller. From May to September he stayed up there by himself, except for tourists and when people brought supplies. His job was to watch for forest fires all summer. I didn't ask, but I really wondered if he had no family.

On the Monday it had rained when we were west of the Continental Divide, Rick said it had snowed on Prairie Reef for seventy-two hours. Peter and Dan, who had been in the valleys to the east side said they had been in a continuous downpour all day. We felt lucky that we had been on the west side that day because the rain had been light most of the day. They were doing a five-day hike.

From where we stood at the top of Prairie Reef we could see Bear Lake down in the valley that we figured is about a four mile hike away. Bear Lake was to our left while in front of us to the east a cliff plunged over a thousand feet down to a valley with a small unnamed lake in it. In this valley there was a large herd of elk grazing and lounging around. Most of them were lying down in the bright midday sun, and to the naked eye they looked like specks down in the valley.

From the top of a high cliff like that it is always tempting to throw rocks over the edge. Elam tossed a few rocks over the edge until Dan spoke up and said how someone he knew was climbing cliffs in Yosemite, Oregon. Apparently there were tourists on top completely unaware of anyone climbing the cliffs. They were throwing rocks over the edge and one of them hit the man that Dan knew and killed him. It was a sobering story and ended all rock throwing after that. You never know what is on the side of the cliff or the bottom even if you can't see them in an uncivilized wilderness.

Rick showed us the remains of a wrecked plane in the valley where the elk were. In the 1970s a pilot lost control while flying among the mountains and crashed his plane to the east of Prairie Reef. Miraculously he had survived the crash. We could only see the wing and a few stray parts of what was left of the plane. It was a grim reminder how in the midst of all the grandeur, majesty, and beauty of the wilderness, it is still an unforgiving place and only the fit survive.

When we finally left the Prairie Reef lookout, three hours later, it felt like we had new friends. Many times since have I regretted not getting Peter and Dan's contact information. I only know that they both live in Bozeman where Peter is a schoolteacher and Dan an economist.

From Prairie Reef we headed north on the rim of the cliff for a couple miles until we came to the lowest spot before the cliff rose again. There was no trail down to the valley where we knew Bear Lake was. Bear Lake was not visible from where we were, but our maps showed it was there and we had seen it from the top of Prairie Reef.

It was a couple hundred feet to the bottom from where we stood to where the cliff ended, and then there was another half mile of steep slope to the valley. We stood there contemplating the washes that went down the sides where rain and water runoff had cut into the cliffs. A snowdrift just below us was oozing water down the sides that made the slippery shale even more treacherous. We dropped down to the snowdrift and threw snowballs at each other. It was neat snowbattling in July.

With Elam picking the way, we eased down the steep slope. It was too steep to go straight down so we went across the side, first one way then the other way on slippery shale. Every step had to be chosen with care.

When we were almost at the bottom there was a crack in the great rocks a couple feet wide that we had to pass through for about fifty feet. Only one person at a time passed through there because of the danger of the persons on top knocking stones loose.

Elam went first. It seemed like a long time until he called up for the next person. We couldn't see him because of the huge boulders on each side of the great crack.

Mervin went next. Slowly he picked his way down the steep shale. This time he took his pack off and tied a rope to it while I held it and slowly let it down.

As I let the rope down, then waited for my turn, I pondered over the situation we had gotten ourselves into. We were in a dangerous situation where a misstep or a slip could result in a terrible fall. But the wilderness was probably not more dangerous than the journey to the wilderness.

As I mulled over this, the call came up that it is my turn. I coiled the rope that I had let down, tied the Klutz to it, and carefully eased my way through the crack with the Klutz sliding in front of me. A couple of places there was just enough of room to squeeze through between the great boulders. At the bottom there was a ledge a couple feet wide with a six foot drop where the cliffs ended and steep shale and rock started. I let the Klutz down over the edge with the rope where Mervin was waiting to grab it. Then I let myself down on my elbows, found a foothold about three feet down, and dropped down to where the cliff ended.

It had taken several hours to come down that terrible cliff, and it felt good to be on slightly more level ground, although it was a lot steeper than what it looked to be from the top. There was still about half a mile of very steep shale and rocks to slide down before we reached the tree line.

Elam had already started and was well ahead of us. We strapped our packs on our backs and slowly eased our way down the steep slope.

There were two ways to go down safely. It was either sitting down on our heels and slide along, or standing up and test every step before putting weight on it. One way was about as strenuous as the other.

At the bottom there were great piles of rock to climb over where we had to be careful how we stepped on them because some of the rocks were very unstable. Not taking time to test each step could send us sprawling with a twisted ankle. But we all made it safely down. I suffered only a few bumps and it felt good to walk in a natural upright position again on horizontal ground the way God intended. Mountain goats and pika God created for the vertical places on earth, while we humans, who naturally walk in the vertical position, are better off on horizontal ground. But still, now that we were safely at the bottom looking back at what we just came down I didn't regret that we had chosen that route. Nevertheless, I wouldn't want to take that route again.

At the tree line there was a spring of fresh water bubbling out of the rocks. Elam had disappeared ahead of us. Mervin was a ways behind me, so I followed a faint trail along the stream into the forest. Bear Lake couldn't be seen, and for about half a mile I went in the direction I thought the lake was. Apparently the trail was only a game trail because soon it petered out. I was alone in the thick forest. I worked my way downhill for I figured the stream would empty into Bear Lake. Here the stream went through a deep ravine, and as I worked my way along something didn't feel quite right. According to my map I should have come to a trail by now.

I checked and rechecked my map. According to the map if I followed the stream it would take me to Bear Lake. But the forest kept becoming thicker, the stream bed was getting really rough, and there was no trail at all. I fought the panicky feeling of being lost. There was no sign of any lake ahead of me and maybe I had somehow started following the wrong stream. The map showed two streams, one was a little farther south than the other that didn't flow into Bear Lake. The sun was already sinking, the forest was becoming gloomy, and I felt very much alone. It was a wild place and my mind was trying to play tricks on me.

I decided to work my way back to where I had started and regroup my direction. I scrambled back up the steep ravine I had come from and hiked about half a mile back to where I had started.

When I came to where the forest thinned out I blew on my whistle. To my amazement, a whistle answered. It was Mervin. He had been puttering around at the spring filling water bottles and drinking from the cold spring. He was raving about how good the water was, and bubbling right out of the ground there was no need for a filter. The strain of not knowing where I was and the scramble back up the hill had made me thirsty. I drank deeply from the spring and was refreshed.

I told Mervin how I had felt lost and decided to come back to regroup. We checked our maps and decided to stay up towards the cliffs that stretched towards Bear Lake and we would be sure to come to the lake. We hiked about a mile along a faint trail and all of a sudden we were at Bear Lake.

It was a beautiful place. The lake itself covered probably about twenty acres and by the color of the water we could see it was very deep. The edges were a greenish tint while in the middle was the deep blue that is a sure sign of deep water in the wilderness. There were two strong streams feeding into the lake on the south side. One of them was the same stream I had been following when I turned back. If I would have followed this stream another half mile I would have come to the lake. There was no visible outlet from the lake. It was like a huge bowl that collected water, then seeped out of the bottom to form streams further down the mountain. It looked like there once had been a huge land slide of shale, rock and dirt, thus forming this strange lake where fresh water flowed into it then seeped out the bottom.

There was no sign of Elam. We whistled and no answer. "Probably looking for a campsite," we decided because we couldn't believe he would have gone further.

We found a nice campsite beside the stream that flowed into the lake and had about decided to camp there when Elam appeared on the far side of the lake. We called for him to come over here but he called us to come over there because he had found a better site. Sure enough, there was more room, although the water supply wasn't as good. We could always depend on Elam to find the best campsites. We had only a quarter mile to the stream if we wanted fresh water.

Wearily we dropped our packs, grateful for the nice campsite that had a fire ring and nice tentsites.

Soon after we arrived at camp I went fishing, hoping to once again have fish for a meal. We knew the lake held fish for we saw them jumping out of the water for flies.

My flyfishing in the wilderness was over for this trip, since I had broken my flyrod at the Chinese Wall. I decided to try my spoon lure on my spinning reel. I fished for an hour or so and didn't get a single bite. Elam and Mervin tried with their flyrods and didn't get anything either. It was maddening. We knew the fish were there but they were not interested in our bait. So we did what all fishermen do when the fish aren't biting. We quit fishing.

## Chapter Seven: Prairie Reef and Bear Lake

Back at the campsite I prepared myself a delicious supper. I had a bagel with peanut butter and honey, Mountain House beef stew with wild garlic added for flavor, a cup of Swiss Miss, a piece of Dove chocolate, topped off with a protein shake and a cup of hot tea.

Sitting around the warm campfire eating supper felt good as the sun set behind the mountains. The air cooled off fast in the gathering twilight. It had been the hardest day yet. We had hiked 11.3 miles over terrain that had been anything but flat. Someone suggested we take a zero day and stay at Bear Lake all day the next day. It didn't take any persuasion for us all to agree, and the matter was settled. Tomorrow we would do no hiking.

We sat around the fire enjoying the warmth, drinking tea, thinking back over the day down those awful cliffs, looking forward to the day off the next day, and enjoying the deep solitude that comes only in the wilderness. I made another entry in my journal by firelight.

Around 10:30 the moon came rising up over the mountains. The moon was full and I went down to the lake to watch it rise. As I sat there on the lakeshore watching the moon rise over the mountain in the distance with trees silhouetted against it, I had a strong urge to howl at the moon. I took a deep breath and bellowed out the longest and the loudest howl I could muster. The sound was incredible as it echoed and reverberated around the valley. I howled again, very much understanding why wolves howl at the moon.

Soon Elam and Mervin joined me and we howled and yelled, each time listening to the echoes reverberate from one mountain to the next. We even yelled at Rick on top of Prairie Reef, hoping he would hear us and know we were safely at Bear Lake four miles away.

We yelled and howled like madmen until we tired of it. It was not like we had close neighbors that would call the cops if we kept them awake.

We stayed at the lake for a while, watching the moon rise higher and higher with its light shining across the water. The fish were jumping out of the water in the moonlight reassuring us that they were still there. Tomorrow we would try again.

The moon was so bright we could see the cliffs we had just come down that afternoon. The snow on top shimmered white in the moonlight.

The deep solitude, the bright moonlight across the lake with the tall majestic mountains on three sides of us, and I again felt as if the wilderness was trying to tell me something; some deep mystery or secret that the mind cannot comprehend and only the heart can grasp. There are no words to describe that feeling. Even the strong word *awesome* is too puny to describe it.

It was a great way to top off a good day.

At 11:45 I wearily crawled into my tent, made another entry in my journal, and sacked out for the night.

The night passed peacefully and the next morning, August 1—the thirteenth day of our hike—dawned clear and chilly. I awoke around 9:00 and just lay there for another half hour staring at the tent ceiling letting my thoughts wander. It was extremely relaxing, lying there in my tent among the pines, listening to the morning sounds of the forest and thinking of many things, but nothing in particular. I very much looked forward to a day with no particular schedule. We intended to fish, swim, wash our clothes, eat, and enjoy this wild spot all to ourselves.

At 9:30 I sat up, made an entry in my journal and crawled out of my tent. Hunger was gnawing at my stomach so before I did much else I had breakfast. I made hot oatmeal with Swiss Miss wild garlic and pecans, string cheese, and a protein shake. I really hoped we could catch some fish out of the lake because my food supply was becoming precariously low for three more days without fish to supplement our diet.

After breakfast I washed my clothes in the lake and hung them up to dry on a makeshift clothesline that we had stretched between two trees. It was a beautiful washday. The Montana sky was the bluest blue, a breeze was stirring with not a cloud in sight. Elam and Mervin had washed their clothes too.

I doctored my blisters on my feet (which had taken a beating the day before on the cliff) and puttered around camp just killing time, until I decided to try and catch fish for lunch.

Since my flyrod was broken I had to use my spinning rod. I used a spoon for bait again.

I was amazed how well the spoon worked. In about an hour I had my limit with a thirteen-, fourteen-, and fifteen-inch lake trout, enough for a meal for each of us. Elam and Mervin didn't have any luck with their flyrods. The banks were very steep and dropped abruptly into the water. It seemed like the fish were out where it was very deep and with their flyrods they couldn't cast as far as I could with my spinning reel. It was awesome hauling in these large, lake trout, but they didn't put up nearly the fight that the river trout did of the same size.

Apparently the strong currents in the river made the river trout much stronger. Even a six-inch river trout could put up quite a fight.

I had a swim before I cleaned my fish for lunch. The water was very cold but I came out of the water refreshed. The bright sun and the breeze soon had me dry.

I cleaned the fish and took them back to camp where we soon had a hot fire going to roast them. They took much longer to cook then the smaller river trout. They were good, but the meat was a little more flaky and didn't quite have the flavor of the river trout. But we weren't complaining because now we would have plenty of food even if we wouldn't catch any more fish. It was a relief to know that we wouldn't have to go hungry.

One of the highlights of the hike was gathering wild food. We had wild fish, wild onions, wild garlic, wild raspberries, and wild huckleberries. There is something about gathering wild food that God put there—which we made no effort to grow—that is very satisfying.

Our lunch was in the middle of the afternoon and by then my clothes had dried. I looked forward to wearing clean, dry clothes once again. The other guys had disappeared to do other things and when I went to check my clothes to see if they were dry I was surprised to find small pebbles in my sock toes.

"Now, how did these get in here?" I asked myself, "Surely a squirrel wouldn't have dropped them in there."

Two of my socks had pebbles in the toes, and when I went to take my pants off the line I found a stone in one of the pockets.

"Very strange," I thought to myself. "What or who would do something like this?" I decided not to say anything. With time the truth would surely come out. I guessed it was just one of those weird things that happen sometimes that can't be explained right away.

My clothes were dry so I chucked the pebbles, pulled my clothes off the line and packed them in my tent to wear the next morning.

Afterward, I went for another swim and lay on the lake shore to dry, soaking in the warm Montana sunshine. I lay too long in the sun and burned my shoulders.

I went fishing again and caught another fifteen-inch trout. I hauled it in, unhooked it, and admired the beautiful fish. I had my limit that day so I released it and watched it swim away in the clear water.

At sundown the fish quit biting. Elam and Mervin were still trying to catch fish with flyrods but none of them caught a single fish.

I had learned a lot about fishing on this trip, but I still felt like I had only touched the tip of the iceberg. I tried to compare a fishing trip to a hunting trip in the wilderness, and I felt I might like hunting better. It would depend on the situation. I was sure hunting would have a lot more pressure. But someday my dream was to hunt elk in a western wilderness.

That night for supper I had potatoes with garlic and beans that Elam had shared. On these last days of our hike we started dividing our food. Elam had plenty of beans.

For dessert I had Dove chocolates, a cup of Swiss Miss, and a cup of hot tea. The first saying on the Dove wrappers was, "Take a run on the wild side." The second wrapper said, "Be proud of your age."

"Very fitting," I thought, as I pondered over the situation and location we were in. We were definitely on the wild side. The area we were in was the wildest country you can find in the Lower Forty-Eight. This was now Saturday night and we hadn't seen a single other person, besides ourselves, since we had left Prairie Reef the day before.

*Bear Lake in the foreground with the cliffs where we had come down from Prairie Reef in the background. The patch of snow at the lowest point is where we had a snow battle.*

91

# Chapter Seven: Prairie Reef and Bear Lake

As for us being proud of our age, I couldn't help but ponder on how fortunate we were. If it weren't for our age we probably wouldn't be here. Who can predict where life will lead us next?

At 10:15 P.M. I crawled into my tent for the night, made an entry in my journal and lay down, mulling over the relaxing day we just had. It had been a good day and the break rejuvenated us.

All of a sudden Elam began raising a big fuss. He kept going off about rocks under his tent. From the sound of things he had gone to lay down and had lain on a couple rocks, one at the foot of the tent and one at the head. He declared they hadn't been there before.

I lay in my sleeping bag laughing to myself and thinking of how what goes around comes around. First I had found a stone on the Klutz. Then I found pebbles in my socks and pants pockets. Now Elam was making a fuss about rocks under his tent. Soon Mervin called out from his tent and said that the night before last, he had found rocks under his tent. Something or someone was playing tricks. I figured with time the truth would come out.

Sunday, Aug. 2, I got up at 6:30 and took a short stroll to the lake. It wasn't as chilly as the previous morning had been and the sky was a little hazy. I figured the haze came from the forest fire north of there because there was not a cloud in sight.

The lake was very beautiful, like a mirror, with not a breath of wind stirring the water. Every now and then a fish jumped, reminding me that they were still there. I sat on the shore trying to absorb the beautiful scene one last time before we leave. It was hard to believe that this was already our fourteenth day in the wilderness and we had only three days and two nights to go. I regretted leaving this beautiful spot, but it was time to move on to the next nice spot.

I filled my water bladder at the creek that flowed into the lake and went for breakfast. For breakfast I had oatmeal with two bags of Swiss Miss and pecans, one string cheese, and a protein shake. I had to limit myself to only one string cheese, but I had plenty of Swiss Miss. It looked like we might be about right for the amount of food we had.

It made a huge difference in the weight of the Klutz. When I went to hoist him onto my back I didn't have to grunt nearly as much anymore. I was especially glad for less weight that morning since my shoulders were slightly burnt from lying in the sun the day before. It wasn't bad, just enough to be slightly irritating.

We planned to hike to the Sun River only eight or ten miles away where we intended to camp for the night. The next few days would be more leisurely as far as distance. We wanted to fish the Sun River yet.

I was the last to leave camp that morning and just as I was leaving I noticed Elam's heavy rope coiled up on a tree. "Oh no," I thought, "He probably forgot to take it along."

I did not feel like packing that heavy rope. But I was sure he wouldn't leave it there on purpose for the next hikers, and besides, if I ever left something lay I would really appreciate it if my fellow hikers would bring it along. So I strapped it onto the Klutz, hoisted him onto my back, and took one long last look at the lake and the beautiful campsite.

Resolutely I turned away, found the trail that led to the Sun River, grateful to have had the privilege to stay at such a wonderful place. We hadn't seen a single other soul since Friday afternoon at Prairie Reef.

From Bear Lake the trail descended for 6.8 miles and 2800 feet to the Sun River.

About an hour after I started on the trail I thought that my pack felt extra heavy considering how little food I had left.

"I wonder if some of those mysterious rocks found their way inside the Klutz again," I thought.

I couldn't believe they would have, but just to make sure, I let the Klutz down and checked him out for hidden rocks. I couldn't find anything unusual. "Must be from Elam's heavy rope or maybe it was from having the day off yesterday," I decided, as I hoisted the Klutz to my back and resumed hiking. Having found rocks in the Klutz and in my clothes had made me suspicious if anything felt unusual.

The trail that took us down to the Sun River descended relentlessly through beautiful pine forests. On our right was Bear Creek that started shortly after we got on the trail. It looked like the water that flowed into Bear Lake seeped underground and formed springs that came up below the lake.

About halfway to the Sun River I met a party of three or four riders heading for Bear Lake. It was the first people we had seen besides ourselves for over forty hours. I nodded a greeting and went on.

# Chapter Eight:
# Camping and Fishing on the Sun River

We reached the Sun River, where Bear Creek emptied into the river around noon. We decided to hike south, upriver for a few miles yet that day. Elam had fished the Sun River in 2012 when they hiked the Bob Marshall Wilderness, and he said there was really good fishing there.

Bear Creek was too wide to step across so we had to take our shoes and socks off to cross. I was glad for my water shoes I had along because I used them time and again.

Just before I came to Bear Creek I met a man who was hiking in some very light canvas shoes. We stopped and chatted for a while.

The conversation turned to blisters. He mentioned how he had so much trouble with blisters when he wears hiking boots. He was with a group of hikers on a five- or six-day hike and the canvas shoes he was wearing he had brought along to wear at creek crossings. But he found that if he wore them to hike it didn't bother his blisters as much. He also said that when his socks get sweaty he'll have a pair hanging on his pack to dry and switch them around every now and then because sweaty socks are the worst thing for blisters. This was something I definitely would try.

We parted, and I crossed Bear Creek grateful for the tip. A lot of people we met on the trail were very willing to share their knowledge and expertise of hiking in the wilderness. Rick, up at Prairie Reef, had given me some moleskin to put on my blisters, someone had shown Elam what wild onions looked like, a fisherman had shown him how the fish go into the brown water at the rapids when the sun shines hot, a forest service man had given me some of his extra flies and told how his father always used spoons and a spinning rod for trout. We met people who lived in the wilderness for weeks at a time, and we met people who were there only a few days. Many of them had a wealth of information to share if we just asked. We learned a great deal and picked up many tips just by talking with the people we met.

Soon after I crossed Bear Creek I sat down in a grove of pines and had my lunch in the cool shade. Elam and Mervin had gone on and I was alone.

Not far from where I had lunch, an outfitter had put up camp beside the river. It was a large camp with an awning stretched between trees for shade. There were large tents, tables to eat off of and chairs to sit on. A short distance away there were horses and packmules tied to trees. It looked like luxury in the wilderness.

It was a beautiful spot, right beside the Sun River and as I hoisted the Klutz to my back and started on the trail, I stopped to chat with them.

It was a group of older people who were out for a few days to enjoy the wilderness and do some fishing. Their guide looked to be about my age. He took care of the horses and mules and did all the packing except his client's personal belongings. They were allowed to pack two bags with a maximum of thirty-five pounds each.

They were friendly, and with true western hospitality, the guide offered me a chair and mixed a glass of tea for me. I was impressed with the friendliness of the people in the wilderness; with the exception of the man that had accused us of stealing his walking stick, I couldn't think of anyone who had been unfriendly. Either the wilderness people were all friendly, or only the friendly people went into the wilderness. I wasn't sure which. Or it could be that the wilderness has a way of mellowing hearts that otherwise sour people become friendly. Once you have been in the wild for days on end without seeing many people, you become ready to talk with outsiders. The wilderness did things to my heart that I knew, once we left, I would never be the same again.

I stayed at the camp for a couple hours and we talked about a great variety of topics. There were four or five older people with the guide. If I remember correctly there were two couples and another man.

We talked about raising hay. In the wilderness they have to feed only certified weed-free hay to the horses. They do not want to bring any noxious weeds into this pristine area.

The conversation turned to politics, then about buffalo; how Ted Turner owned huge tracts of land where they needed to thin the buffalo herds and the local Indians wanted to claim them as their own. Apparently the Indians thought they would have the right to these buffalo on private land. It sounded like a big stink.

Then they told stories of how buffaloes attacked people. Some of the tourists did stupid things; like this one lady who wanted to take a selfie with a buffalo and it attacked her. Many tourists think the buffalo is a big tame creature. They may not be as wild as deer or elk, but to stand beside one to take a selfie is crazy.

It was an entertaining afternoon, sitting there visiting with locals and hearing about the things they deal with. When I decided it's time to move on and grabbed the Klutz and hoisted him onto my back; one of the older men commented drily, "I vaguely remember when I used to be able to do that." This man made the most humorous remarks in the driest way. I guessed him to be in his seventies.

As I left their camp I thought of how privileged I had been to meet such nice people. It was a great way to spend a Sunday afternoon in the wilderness.

I followed trail number 202 along the Sun River for about three and a half miles. It was a little rolling for about two miles until I came to a long flat area about a mile long. The place was called Pretty Prairie and used to be an airstrip back before the Bob Marshall Wilderness was closed to all vehicle traffic. There were no trees on this straight stretch of trail and the sun beat down hot as I began the long hike across the prairie.

Tall grass grew on each side of the trail, and when I had hiked about a quarter mile I heard strange squeaking in the grass beside the trail. On and on the squeaking went. I poked my walking stick into the tall grass, trying to figure out what it was. I was startled when I saw it was a snake trying to swallow a mouse. I couldn't see the mouse's head as I beat the snake with my stick until it spit out the mouse and went slithering away into the tall grass. I couldn't find the mouse right away, but it kept right on squeaking even after the snake disappeared. I poked around in the tall grass until I saw the mouse sitting there with a wet front end, crying its head off.

"Poor thing," I thought, "that was a close call."

I let the mouse go. I figured if I saved its life that close it may as well enjoy it. Besides, I didn't have to worry that it would ever get into my barns anyway, and our next campsite was a couple miles away.

*Pretty Prairie where the snake was swallowing the mouse.*

*Pretty Prairie station.*

It made me ponder over the unpredictableness of life as I walked away from the scene. If I wouldn't have come along at that precise moment that mouse would never have seen the light of day again. On the other hand, why didn't I feel sorry for the snake because I just got done robbing it of a meal? Now the snake would have to start all over to get a meal. If snakes have feelings, it probably felt like I do when I have a fish on the line and I'm anticipating a delicious meal, when just as I have the fish at the bank of the river it comes loose and swims away. Whatever the snake's feelings, I still didn't regret releasing the mouse, literally from the jaws of death. It was impressed upon me how in the wilderness some animals must die so others can live.

The sky kept becoming more hazy from the fires up north but the sun still shone hot through the haze. When I came to the end of the prairie, I entered more pine forests where it was cooler. It was another mile or so until I met Elam and Mervin. They had found a good campsite by the river.

Elam said there was a forest service station at the edge of Pretty Prairie where a worker had just arrived. I went up to the cabin to have a chat with him. They were usually friendly and willing to share a wealth of information.

When I came to the cabin he was sitting on the porch with his feet propped up reading a book. He had turned his horses out in a makeshift pasture that was made of polywire stretched between trees and portable posts. He was friendly and we had a good chat.

He said he had worked for the forest service for thirty-three years. He hauled supplies around with his horses. We chatted for about an hour or so. While we were visiting a flock of seven grouse went parading right past the front porch.

He kept bells on one of his horses that rang as the horse grazed, "As long as the bells keep ringing," he said, "I can sleep at night, but when they quit ringing I wake up. Usually when I can't hear the bell anymore it means the horse has gotten through the fence and wandered away. Then I have to go search for him."

We talked about the different types of horses that are good in the mountains. He preferred the morgans. "The morgans have very good endurance in the mountains," he declared.

He talked about how he goes elk hunting every year and always shoots a cow. "Their meat is so much better than a bull," he stated.

# Chapter Eight: Camping and Fishing on the Sun River

"I suppose you have your bull racks already," I commented.

"I never hunted elk for their antlers," he said.

It was surprising to me that there are still hunters that hunt only for the meat and don't care how big the antlers are. But resident elk tags are inexpensive in Montana and if you would live in the mountains for thirty-some years, I'm sure the thrill of chasing elk would wear off. When I took that in consideration it made sense that he hunted only for the meat.

As we sat there talking, a boy of about seventeen came walking up the trail with a flyrod in his hands.

"Have you caught anything?" my new friend inquired.

"Only a couple," the young boy said.

Apparently he had released them again because I didn't see any fish.

"This is my assistant," the ranger explained.

The ranger had a radio with him and he showed me how they relay messages from one spot to the next. Soon a call came in from Rick at Prairie Reef. It was nothing really important, but hearing Rick's voice over the two-way made me want to tell him where we were. But I didn't say anything because I figured they probably wouldn't want too much outside chatter. Later I wished I would have said something, but the call was over before I had the chance to think a lot about it.

I left the cabin and went back to our campsite by the river. When I was setting up my tent a weasel scampered across a log about thirty feet away. I didn't know what else it was. It had a long narrow body and a furry tail that was about as long as its body. The other guys were nowhere to be seen.

Later we cooked our evening meal around the fire, thinking back over the day. Elam had gone about a mile farther to a spot on the Sun River that had been an excellent fishing hole three years before. But the river had changed since then and the hole wasn't there anymore.

We had hiked 11.9 miles that day, quite a bit farther than I had expected. The trail had been relatively easy though, and I had met some interesting people that day.

The Dove wrapper message that night was, "The more you praise and celebrate your life, the more there is to celebrate." Some of those messages were about as good as the candy itself.

At 8:45 I crawled into my tent and made another entry in my journal.

The next morning, August 3, 2015, the fifteenth day of our hike, I got up at 6:15. The sky was hazy from faraway forest fires and it was cold and breezy, with the temperature at forty-five degrees. The sun hadn't come up over the mountain yet while we huddled around the fire trying to warm up and complained how cold it was. Although it wasn't as cold as some mornings had been, we were camped beside the river between the mountains where the wind blew along the river picking up cool damp air from the water and hurling it right into our faces. We knew we shouldn't complain because the temperature often hit ninety degrees by late afternoon. But that seemed like a long way off and it was cold!

For breakfast I had two string cheeses, oatmeal with Swiss Miss, and a protein shake.

Afterward I went fishing and caught two fish for 9:30 break. Then I wrapped up camp and went fishing again. The fishing was phenomenal. I caught a thirteen-incher, then a twelve-incher and kept the twelve-incher for lunch. There were deep pools and shallow, swift moving water to fish in. I was astonished how well my spoon bait worked for I caught one fish after the next. Eventually they quit biting, and by that time it was around noon. I cooked the twelve-incher for lunch. It was ever so good. There is nothing like fresh mountain trout cooked over a campfire with a little salt.

After lunch I slung the much lighter Klutz on my shoulders and headed back towards Bear Creek. We went back past the ranger cabin— the ranger was long gone with his horses—and back across Pretty Prairie where I had interrupted the snake's lunch. We followed the river to where the outfitters camp had been the day before, and then I took a break. I had pulled ahead of Elam and Mervin and they were nowhere in sight.

The outfitter was gone. The only sign that he had been there was trampled grass and a fresh campfire site. I dropped the Klutz against a tree, leaned back, and took a snooze in the shade away from the hot afternoon sun. It was a hot day with temperatures up towards ninety degrees. I wondered why we complained about the cold that morning. The sky was cloudless but hazy from the smoke of the forest fires in the north. The haze helped that it wasn't quite as hot.

I pulled my hat over my eyes and dozed for a while until Mervin and Elam came along. The river looked good for fishing so I pulled my rod out of the Klutz with the spoon bait, dropped down the steep bank to the river, and cast. The fish were biting, and I caught one after the next. I lost count of how many I caught. I had my limit for the day so I released them all.

The fish on the Sun River were more feisty than the ones we caught in the South Fork of the Flathead. The Flathead has mostly cutthroat trout, while here there were rainbows, cutbow (a cross of rainbow and cutthroat) and brown trout. When a six-inch rainbow trout hits your line, it is *bam*, and off they go. I knew without a doubt that something hit my line when a rainbow struck.

As I was enjoying myself catching fish, a party of riders rode in. I couldn't see them because of the high banks, but I heard someone talking and when I looked up over the river bank they were there talking with Mervin.

I fished for a while until the fish quit biting. I scrambled up the bank to the Klutz where the riders were setting up camp. There was around six of them, and they used mules to pack their stuff. They were from Minnesota and had trucked their own horses and mules all the way to the Bob Marshall Wilderness for a five-day riding trip.

They were friendly, typical country folk. I chatted with them awhile before I went on.

Two of the men used to milk cows. One of the former dairy men now had some beef cows and did welding. I found that interesting for that was exactly what I was doing after quitting the dairy business. He also made spurs out of old rasps.

"What do you work?" one of the men asked me.

"I have beef cows and weld," I replied. "I weld parts for the Well Built wagons built by Stoltzfus Manufacturing."

"Those are good wagons," one of the men declared. "Much better than some of the cheap wagons you can buy."

I was astonished how he knew the name right away. "Small world we live in," I thought.

We chatted on for a while. They came to the Bob Marshall Wilderness quite often for horseback rides.

One year when they were there, their trip was cut short by forest fires. There was great clouds of smoke, they could all see the fire come over the ridges towards them, and they knew they had to get out, now! That year they did not have a good trip. The fires ruined it for them. With the plume of smoke we had seen from the top of Prairie Reef, and now the hazy sky from the same fire, I understood why a forest fire would ruin a trip in the wilderness.

I was grateful that so far we didn't have to deal with any forest fires.

I left their camp marveling at the coincidence of meeting other former dairymen in the wilderness. I wondered at the odds of meeting other farmers in the wilderness like that. "Maybe those are the kind of folks that go for the wild parts," I thought. "That would raise the odds a lot."

At any rate, it was great meeting fellow farmers in such a place while we had so much in common. After milking cows for so many years, it seems trips like this come naturally.

Where Bear Creek flowed into the Sun River it looked like good fishing. I pulled out my rod and went fishing. The fish were still biting, and I spent another hour or so catching and releasing fish after fish. I never tired of fishing while the fish were biting.

It was late in the afternoon when I crossed Bear Creek and took trail number 202 that followed the Sun River to our last campsite on the very edge of the great Bob Marshall Wilderness. It was just over a mile to where Elam said a good campsite was where the Sun River went down some falls and rapids.

The trail to the campsite was moderate and went up and down with the rolling foothills along the river. The mountains weren't as high as we headed from the wilderness toward the plains. The Sun River was around 5000 feet, with peaks reaching between 6500 and 7000 feet on each side of the river.

Just before we came to the campsite that Elam had chosen, there was a sign that said we are now entering the Lewis and Clark National Forest. Officially we were leaving the wilderness. But we still had a seven-mile hike along the Sun River that flowed into the Gibson Reservoir until we reached Mortimer Gulch where we had scheduled Dave to meet us the next day.

I had mixed feelings when I thought of leaving the great Bob Marshall Wilderness that had done so much for me, and heading back to civilization. But we had been on the trails for fifteen days, our food was running low, and it was time to face the world of civilization again. I knew I would never be the same again. The wilderness with its vast distance, the solitude, the wildlife, the phenomenal fishing, the people we had met, the nighttime stargazing and moonlighting, had touched me in places that cannot be seen. Often I thought of the words of Jack Rich, "When all is said and done it recharges the part that cannot be seen." Finding the right words to explain what the wilderness taught me and did for me is difficult.

The campsite Elam had chosen for our last night out was a beautiful spot in a grove of pines right beside the river. The river dropped down sharply, tumbled down fast rapids and short waterfalls into deep pools as it left the wilderness and flowed another seven miles into the Gibson Reservoir where it was stored to be used for irrigation.

From our campsite we had to drop down twenty or thirty feet over the rocks to get to the deep pool below the falls. Elam and Mervin soon had their daily limit of fish, and since I had caught my limit that morning I had to go without fish for supper. I wasn't complaining, but I did wish I could have had some. Elam and Mervin seemed to have no inclination to share, and I was too proud to beg.

I spent some time fishing the pools around the rapids and caught quite a mess of fish. I was amazed at how well my spoon lure was still working. The treble hook had only one hook left, but it was still plenty of hook to catch those feisty rainbows when they struck. I didn't tire of the thrill when a rainbow struck.

I worked my way up among the white water of the rapids, casting into the pools around the rapids and getting hits almost every time I cast for the first time into a pool.

As I worked my way up among the rapids and falls, a flock of redheaded ducks treated me to a spectacular sight of nature at its best. There was a mother duck and about half a dozen of her young swimming among the pools where I was fishing. Soon they floated to a spot in the river where the water slid down over the rocks almost straight down for three or four feet. There wasn't much white water there and they slid down on the water single file, just like a water slide. Then they went right through the pool where I was fishing, no more than ten feet away.

I forgot all about fishing as I watched them approach the next slide where there was white water rushing through a narrow chute with water spraying all around. I watched in amazement as they calmly approached the white water. Just as the lead duck came to the white water and I thought that she surely would get dashed against the rocks, she flapped her wings, flew and hopped over the white water down to the next pool with all the half grown ducks following her, flapping their wings as they went. It looked like they knew exactly what they were doing and it looked like fun. For a moment I wished I could be a duck.

I resumed fishing, caught a few more fish, then headed back to camp,

*The Sun River rapids and falls where the Redheaded ducks were.*

grateful for the opportunity to witness and be part of such an amazing spectacle. We never knew what would happen or what we would see next.

Back at camp we swapped food and cooked a meal. Elam and Mervin feasted on fish while I had to settle with noodles and some of the dried vegetables Elam had given me.

As I was waiting for my food to cool off it started raining. It didn't rain hard, just enough to make things wet and chase us into our tents to eat the food. There was thunder in the distance.

By 9:30 I was done eating, made another entry in my journal, and was ready to hit the sack one more time before we ended our trip.

It had been a good day. We hadn't pushed it and only covered 6.2 miles. But the fishing had been excellent and I wasn't complaining.

I entered my tent and pondered over the last few weeks; how this had been my home every night for fifteen nights in a row. I had worked out a system. First I needed a flat spot free from rocks and roots for a tentsite. Once I found a suitable spot I pulled my tent out of my pack and set it up on the flat spot. Next I unwrapped my sleeping mat and laid it on the floor of the tent. Then I pulled my sleeping bag out of the Klutz, shook out the rumples, and laid it on the sleeping mat. My shoes and socks went at the foot of the tent, and my waterbladder went outside the tent flap beside the bearspray in easy reach. The Klutz I lay on his side in the tent; my pants and shirt went inside my sleeping bag with me; my sweater I folded up for a pillow; my journal, flashlight, pocket testament and first aid kit went beside my shoulders outside my sleeping bag, while my binoculars I stored in the point of the tent just past my head. I had enough of room to sit up, roll around, and fully stretch out while the tent kept me high and dry from bad weather.

My tent had become a haven for me. The smell didn't bother me at all anymore, and I had become so comfortable on the mat in my sleeping bag that I had dreamed of being at home in my own bed several times. The dreams had been so vivid that when I awoke it had taken a little time for the reality to soak in my foggy brain that I was still in my tent out in the great Bob Marshall Wilderness.

After sitting and lying on the ground for fifteen days, I almost forgot how plush seats felt anymore.

The next morning, Tuesday, Aug. 4, 2015, the last day of our hike I got up at 6:00. It was a little warmer than the morning before, the sky was overcast, but no rain, and the temperature was around fifty degrees.

I went fishing down at the deep hole below our camp. I cast my spoon lure beside an overhanging rock and *bam*, a thirteen-inch trout struck on the first cast. I hauled it in, pulled it up on the rock I was standing on, and admired the beautiful rainbow. I was sorely tempted to just once eat a fish over the limit, but no, I wanted to respect the game laws. These laws are usually enacted for a reason.

I unhooked the fish, dropped it back in the deep pool, and watched it swim back to freedom. I resumed fishing and within half an hour I had caught an eleven inch rainbow and a nine inch brown trout for breakfast. I was hungry and the fish were good with the last of my breakfast food. After breakfast Elam and I hiked back across the wilderness boundary and hiked up a small mountain called Sun Butte. Mervin had a sore foot that was acting up, so he stayed back at camp to pack up and rest for the seven-mile hike to the trail head.

It was a two-and-a-half-mile hike up to the top of Sun Butte where we were right on the very edge of the wilderness. At 5700 feet, the 700 foot climb to the top seemed like a walk in the park compared to the 3000 feet or more of climbing to the tops of Pagoda and Prairie Reef peaks had been. We weren't carrying our packs either (just some water) which made a big difference, too.

Although the climb wasn't as strenuous the views from the top were spectacular. To the east we could see the plains and the wheat fields that we had seen from Prairie Reef. They were much closer now, and we expected to reach them by the end of the day.

A private ranch was located against the Sun River directly below us. It was owned by a family whom the government had paid with land instead of money for serving in the military. They owned a lot of land bordering the wilderness. There was a house and barn with horses in the pastures surrounding the barn. There was a guest house or hotel where the people stayed who came to the ranch to ride. It looked like a dude ranch where you could rent horses and have a place to stay close to the wilderness.

It felt surreal, looking down on civilization from our vantage point on top of Sun Butte. For over two weeks we hadn't seen a single permanent dwelling—except for ranger cabins—and seeing houses, barns, and people living there made me feel funny. I wasn't sure if I liked it.

Behind us to the north and west the unbroken wilderness stretched away.

*View to the north from the top of Sun Butte with the North Fork of the Sun River below us. The haze in the sky is smoke from forest fires.*

107

*At the very edge of the wilderness looking east*
*from the top of Sun Butte with the Sun River below us.*

*At the far end of Gibson reservoir*
*with the Sun River flowing through the dry lakebed.*

*Trail cut on the side of the cliff with Gibson reservoir down on the right.*

*Gibson reservoir Dam in the background. Note the high water mark.*

# Chapter Eight: Camping and Fishing on the Sun River

For centuries the mountains had stood there, unchanged in the midst of a changing world. If the Lord tarries, they will stand unchanging for centuries to come.

I think one of the reasons why the mountains and wilderness have such a strong magnetic appeal is because they offer a form of stability in an unstable world. The world is full of turmoil, hurt, bitterness, and strife, while the mountains stand there, unmovable, unchanged and stable. But they require respect, because if you don't respect them for what they are they will get you. You can climb the highest peak and feel like you have conquered it, but when you come down, the mountain will stay there, unmovable, unchanging and as high as ever, while we go back to our lives better than we were before.

I like thinking of God like that; unmovable, unchangeable, and stable. We can search for Him, study His word, talk to Him, and be close to Him, be better because of Him, and know Him. But we will never be able to understand Him completely and know His mind. Just like a mountain; He requires respect and is not mocked.

I stood there trying to absorb the view and contemplating on the fact that this was the last day of our hike. The wilderness had done a lot for me in ways that are hard to describe. I understood why folks go to the wilderness for solace and healing. Jesus himself, often went into the wilderness to pray, and once he fasted in the wilderness for forty days and nights.

Elam had left to go back down before I did. I took one last look around, resolutely turned back, and followed Elam down to our campsite.

Mervin was almost done packing up camp when we arrived. We left camp at 11:00, took the trail that led to Gibson Reservoir through the Lewis and Clark National Forest away from the great Bob Marshall Wilderness. The trail followed the Sun River and went right through the ranch we had seen from the top of Sun Butte.

Just before we came to the ranch we met a man on horseback leading a couple pack mules. We waved and nodded a greeting as he passed by.

"Where are you heading to?" Elam asked.

"I'm taking supplies to Big Prairie," he replied, as we watched the heavily laden mules behind him.

The trail passed through the ranch, then followed the Sun River all the way to Gibson reservoir. It was a nice trail, heavily used, with the river on our right, while mountains and cliffs rose high on our left. In some areas the trail

*Water gushing out of the pipes at Gibson reservoir dam.*

was out on the side of the cliffs with a wall straight up to the left and a sheer drop down to the lake hundreds of feet below us on our right.

I had gotten ahead of Elam and Mervin and was traveling alone on the cliff trail when I noticed a long packtrain behind me. The packtrain was still a couple miles behind me where the flats started (right where the river flowed into the reservoir) when I first saw him. It was a lone cowboy riding a horse in the front, leading a second horse with a pack and nine more mules behind the second horse, all loaded with packs, except the last one had only a saddle on its back.

Slowly they caught up to me. They passed me on the cliffs and I had just room enough to step to the side to let them pass.

"Where are you headed to?" I called out as I stepped to the side.

"I'm taking supplies to the Sun Canyon lodge," he replied as he passed me, while each mule stepped away from me as far as they could on the edge of the cliff. They had no intention of coming closer than possible to a grizzled man with a dirty pack and smelly clothes.

"Typical mules," I muttered to myself, while I watched them disappear around a bend among the cliffs.

111

*The vast fields of Montana.*

As I watched them disappear around the bend I marveled how in this day and age with all its advanced modes of travel that there were still people who depended on packtrains like that to survive.

The picture of that long packtrain would have been the same two hundred years before. I appreciated anew the laws and effort that kept areas like this so pristine.

I trudged on among the cliffs trying to absorb as much of the scenery as possible. The Klutz on my back was much lighter with not much left except my gear. I had my lunch back where the Sun River flowed into the reservoir. I ate the last of my granola bars, the trail mix and nuts were gone, all my noodles and hot meals were gone. The only food I had left was one or two Dove chocolates, half a bagel, a little peanut butter, two packs of Swiss Miss, and a little salt in my shaker. Not even enough for a full meal without fish.

At 2:30 I reached the trail's end at the parking lot by Mortimer Gulch. It made me feel funny seeing blacktop, cars, and civilization again. For sixteen days we hadn't seen a single car or truck, or even blacktop. I wasn't sure how I was supposed to feel. One thing I knew, I would never be the same again. The wilderness did things to me like no other place ever did.

We had much to be thankful for. We hiked eleven miles on the last day including the hike up to Sun Butte, which made a total of 146.1 miles. We averaged 9.13 miles per day. Except for blisters, sore muscles and feet, no one got hurt. We were blessed with nice weather, no near forest fires, no attacks from bears, wolves,or mountain lions. We had good reason to be grateful for the protection God provided. The only time I felt any real danger was the time we climbed down the cliffs just before Bear Lake. But we made it through safely and all was well.

Now I was back to civilization. Elam and Mervin hadn't shown up yet so I sat down in the shade and scribbled in my journal for a while.

There were modern restrooms nearby, a luxury we hadn't known for over two weeks. Some of the ranger cabins had primitive outhouses that we sometimes used. I learned that we could live with a lot less if we just would. But it seems the more man has available the more he uses. That was another thing the wilderness taught me; I can often make do with what I have or improvise with what is available.

There was still no sign of Mervin and Elam so I walked around to the lower parking lot. I found them at the boat launch with Dave and his girlfriend.

We put our almost empty packs in the back of Dave's truck, climbed in the back seats, with Dave and his girlfriend in the front. Sitting on plush seats felt strange after sixteen days of sitting on the ground, logs, or rocks.

Dave turned the key, the engine started, and we began our long trip home, away from the great Bob Marshall Wilderness. The hike was over.

# Chapter Nine: Homebound Journey

We circled around the dam to the bottom side where Dave wanted to show us where the water came out. It was a short walk from the parking lot to where the water came through the concrete dam in great big pipes. The water poured out of the pipes, sprayed a mist all around and went tumbling angrily down the river.

Dave said the reservoir was used to irrigate 8000 areas of farmland out on the plains. There was only a week's worth of water left in the reservoir. In the West, farmland is priced by the amount of water that is available for irrigation. Often they have disputes between the cities and the farmers for water rights. Now with much of the West in a drought the water wars only become worse.

We watched the water pour out of the great pipes for a while, marveling at the extreme pressure. Soon we headed back to the parking lot, got back on our plush seats and headed out to the plains.

The road took us out to the plains where the mountains stopped abruptly and gave way to large cattle ranches and the wheat fields that we had seen way back on top of Prairie Reef. Seeing the fields, cattle, and wide open spaces stirred my farmer's heart. It was great to be among beef cattle and crops again.

We headed for the nearest town where we stopped and treated ourselves to ice cream. The ice cream took the edge off of our appetites while we headed to Dave's house to take showers and clean up before heading to a place for a steak supper.

It was time to clean up. My only pair of pants that I had along on the hike were busting at the seams around the ankles. I looked in the mirror in Dave's bathroom and I was shocked at the grimy, dark, grizzled face that stared back at me. I hadn't shaved or showered since Rexford. We had washed ourselves in the creeks and rivers a few times, but with no soap or hot water we couldn't get off all the dirt. Besides, we just got dirty right away anyway.

The dirt didn't hurt us any. In fact, I felt healthier and more physically (and mentally) fit than I had for years. The dirt that we had on us was good, clean, wilderness dirt.

Our travel bags had arrived safely with clean clothes that we had shipped from Kalispell. I took out clean clothes, my razor and soap, stripped off my dirty clothes, jumped in the shower with hot water and watched sixteen days of dirt and grime run down the drain. I stepped out of the shower feeling clean and civilized once more. There was one major job yet before I felt completely civilized. Dave had said we could use his razors so I grabbed a new, sharp, triple bladed razor, applied shaving cream to my face, and attacked two and a half weeks' growth of beard. I chopped and hacked away until my face was as smooth as a freshly mowed field of hay. Now I felt more like myself.

Elam and Mervin cleaned up too before we went to the steakhouse for a meal.

We went to a place called Elk Country where we had steak and mountain oysters with all the fixings. Seldom do I eat that much in one sitting.

With our stomachs full we headed for a hotel in Shelby where we stayed for the night. The train was due to leave Shelby at 11:43 A.M.

Shelby is a typical Western town with Main Street running the length of town. There were stores with souvenirs along Main Street, bars, and the ever-present casino. A major freight line runs through Shelby, and the great freight trains rumbled and clattered past our hotel as we tried to sleep.

The hotel air left a lot to be desired and felt warm and stuffy after being used to the fresh, clean mountain air for so long. We only booked one room so I slept on a cot while Elam and Mervin shared the bed. The cot was nice and soft, but I didn't sleep any better than when I slept on the ground in the Bob Marshall Wilderness. The air was so stuffy we opened a window for fresh air. It was loud from all the traffic and trains but at least we had a little more fresh air. I would take the noise of a creek or waterfall any night over traffic or engines. But all vacations must end when we need to get back to civilization and all the noise that goes with it.

Wednesday, August 5, we got up and had breakfast at the motel. We had to break the routine of camp life now and I didn't like it. Hiking and camping for days on end became a lifestyle and now we had to change it.

Out train wasn't due to leave Shelby until 11:43 and I was bored. I walked around Shelby, looking at the freight trains, browsing in the stores and shops, wishing our train would come.

I walked down to the station where I saw a man lying on the bench outside the station. "Must be homeless," I thought as I passed him and went on checking out the stores that were around.

At the Chamber of Commerce they had a stuffed mountain lion hanging on the wall. Below it there was a newspaper article telling how this lion had roamed the streets of Shelby some years before. The authorities tracked it down, ended up shooting it, and mounting it for display. It was a reminder that we were in the West.

Our train arrived early and as we boarded I noticed the man that had been sleeping on the bench was boarding too. Soon the conductor (who was a big man at least six feet tall and probably two hundred fifty pounds) came along and said to the man, "I hope you can keep yourself in control and not drink too much this time."

"I was not drinking," the man retorted, as we boarded the train.

"Well, just make sure you keep yourself under control," the big conductor admonished firmly, but not unkindly.

Apparently the man had gotten into a fight, had been kicked off the train the day before and had slept at the station all night. He settled into a seat behind us and we didn't hear a peep out of him all the way to Chicago.

At exactly 11:43 the train pulled away from Shelby and we began our long journey home.

As we passed through the wheat, barley and oat fields that we had seen from the top of Prairie Reef the harvest was in full swing. Thousands and thousands of acres in cropland. The fields were so vast a forty-foot combine looked small in those fields. Three weeks before when we had passed through, the crops were just beginning to ripen. It was interesting to see the harvest in full swing now. It was great seeing all the farmland again.

When we reached North Dakota the train was two hours behind schedule already. The train lost a lot of time in Central Montana because of the freight train wrecks several weeks before. We passed a place where a string of oil tankers lay on their sides. It looked like they had quite a spill. The tracks

*Wrecked oil tankers along the tracks*

weren't so good there, and as a precaution, Amtrak sped along at ten miles an hour for a stretch.

At 10:30 P.M. I entered in my journal that we are now in North Dakota. North Dakota has a booming oil business with a lot of oil pumps, trucks, and drilling rigs that we could see as the train sped by. At the oil fields we were past the bad section of tracks and traveling at normal speeds.

The landscape constantly changed as we headed east. There were huge ranches where cattle grazed; some areas grew oil pumps that nodded at us as we passed them by; there were enormous fields of crops; there were bluffs and scrubland; there were towns and cities with many people as we rolled on east. I didn't tire of watching the ever-changing landscape.

Thursday morning, August 6, 2015, I made an entry in my journal at 8:10 A.M. I had a decent night's sleep but still felt cooped up on the train.

As we neared St. Paul, Minnesota, we saw a lot of irrigated corn and soybean fields. The wheat harvest was done, the cornfields looked like they just came into tassle and most of the soybean fields looked good. This was about as far north as corn gets grown, and it was interesting to see how farmers operated in the different areas as the train rolled on.

Even from the train the agricultural atmosphere and honesty could be felt. Travelling through the cities with all the graffiti, noise, high rises, dirt, grime, and people everywhere, made me appreciate wide open spaces. After sixteen days of rugged physical exercise, I felt very cooped up.

I spent a lot of time in the lounge car, reading, eating, watching the scenery as we rolled past, and meeting new friends. I got into a conversation with two middle-aged sisters that were sitting across the aisle from me. Their names were Rhonda and Renae. They grew up on a farm in Washington and had a Mennonite background. They both were schoolteachers. Rhonda taught writing, and Renae was married to a man that worked for the largest onion seed dealer in the world where they sell six million dollars worth of seed every year. They were traveling to Chicago to see a relative.

We talked for hours about a lot of in-depth subjects. We talked about the plan of salvation, how the only way to be saved was through faith in Jesus Christ. They were relieved to hear that because they were under the impression that the Amish believe they are saved through their plain clothes and lifestyle. It hurts when outside people think that is what we believe. Plain clothes and a plain lifestyle is not our salvation but how we choose to live. Traveling outside of our close-knit communities always makes me appreciate the value of our lifestyle and the way we choose to live.

Renae gave me her address and phone number and when we parted we agreed to stay in touch. Before we parted they treated me to lunch where we got into an interesting conversation about writing books and why some authors are so much better than others. As we neared Chicago we went back to our seats to our luggage with the promise to stay in touch.

We arrived in Chicago at 6:45 P.M. and just missed the Pittsburgh train by five minutes. A great crowd of people came off the train and I caught a glimpse of Rhonda walking alongside the train while we still were seated ,waiting for our turn to get off. When we finally came off, Renae and Rhonda had disappeared and I saw them no more.

Our train was two hours late and we had expected to miss the Pittsburgh train. We were stuck in Chicago for twenty-four hours. We searched for a hotel and found a luxurious place called the Dewitt with a rooftop restaurant, bellhops who carried our luggage, and an air about it that declared money everywhere. Our rooms had soft beds, full showers, and windows where we could see right out at other high rises of Chicago. Quite a contrast to the mountains and clean air we had been used to. I didn't like it.

After we had settled in our room we went out to eat at an upscale restaurant called Hurray Harry's. The food was okay, but expensive. I was ready to get back to the real world.

We got back to the hotel around 11:00. I slept well until morning.

Friday morning we got up and had breakfast at a famous restaurant called Lou Mitchell's. It was a good place to eat, but again, there were people everywhere. After breakfast we went up the Willis Tower where there were so many people we had to wait in line to go in, wait in line to go up, wait in line to go out on the glass deck, and wait in line to go down. With 25,000 visitors a day, waiting is part of it.

At the top they have a glass observation deck where we could stand on a glass floor with glass sides around us, over a thousand feet above the street. It was quite an experience even if the waiting with people all around drove me about crazy. Unlike the West there is no solitude in Chicago.

Next we toured the Money Museum at the Federal Reserve Bank. They had bills on display dating back hundreds of years. There was a large glass cube that had one million one-dollar bills in it. The cube was around six feet square and weighed about a ton.

There was a briefcase filled with a million dollars worth of one hundred dollar bills and another glassed in box filled with a million dollars in twenty dollar bills.

There were bills under a glassed area where they showed what to look for in counterfeit bills. It was interesting and educational.

We went through the public library next. At ten stories high it was a huge place. Each floor had a different category. One floor had old books, another floor was history, some floors had a lot of open space where people just were. It was unlike any other library I ever was. We didn't spend much time in there for we wanted to see the Navy Pier.

The Navy Pier is beside Lake Michigan where they had places to eat, boat rides, merry-go-rounds, a Ferris wheel and other rides. There were people everywhere.

We toured a greenhouse where they had lots of exotic plants that I had never seen before.

When we were done touring the greenhouse it was late afternoon and time to head back for the train station. We had walked six or seven miles by then. Mervin's foot was hurting him and we didn't have time to walk back so we hailed a taxi to take us back. Going back with the taxi among all the traffic and people made me ready to be at home.

We went for supper when we came back to the station. I was hungry for pizza so I went to a pizza shop and had three slices of pizza. The pizza was good, but I was tired of all the people.

After stuffing myself with pizza I went back to the station. I went to the locker room to get my luggage when surprise, there was cousin Elmer Fisher and his wife on their way home from visiting in Colorado. It was neat meeting someone I knew among all the strangers rushing around the train station.

It was Friday night and there were people everywhere. When the commuter trains came in I was reminded of a cattle chute when people poured out of the trains, up the steps, and came swarming into the station.

Our train left at 6:40, right on time, and headed for Pittsburgh.

I went to the lounge car for a drink and sat at one of the tables. There was a middle-aged man sitting across from me who went by the name of Lawson. He was moving from California to Philadelphia and was travelling by train. We visited awhile until he asked me if I'd be interested in playing a two-person game called Jaipur.

"Sure," I said, "I'd be glad to." I was grateful for a way to pass the time. Jaipur is a game of trading and selling; things like leather, linen, spices, silver, gold and gems. We got carried away. The lounge car emptied and it was past midnight when we finally quit. It was a great pastime and made for a short night.

I never got Lawson's phone number or address and he'll probably be another person I'll never see again on earth. We met so many nice people on our trip that touched our lives for just a little while, that there is no way we would have the time to follow up on all of them later. I wondered how many people whom we had touched would remember us later and think back with warm feelings about the experience. Life is an experience and it is up to us to choose to look for the good or the bad.

Saturday, August 8, 2015, we arrived in Pittsburgh at 5:30 A.M. We were sitting in the station waiting for our train (that was due at 7:30) when a woman, who was sitting on a chair beside us, passed out and fell out of her chair onto the floor. There was a flurry of commotion as people rushed to her side to help her. Mervin had taken CPR training recently and he tapped her shoulder to revive her. She regained consciousness and someone helped her on her chair. She said she had a medical condition that caused this and it just happened that her husband had gone for a bite to eat.

It was amazing how people wanted to help. One man came and asked her if she wanted a drink. He seemed to have medical training and asked her questions that sounded like he knew what he was doing. Another woman sat beside her and gave her emotional support like only a woman can. These were complete strangers who happened to be at the same place at the same time and were willing to help someone in need with no thought of a reward. It strengthened my faith in humanity.

We decided to get a bite to eat before our train left. We asked Elmer and his wife to watch our luggage while we walked about a mile until we found a sandwich shop that was open early on a Saturday morning. The bagel sandwich was good, and with our appetites satisfied we headed back to the station.

When we came back to the station, there were emergency vehicles there. Apparently the woman who had passed out needed medical care. We didn't hear any details.

Our train was in the depot. We quickly grabbed our luggage and boarded the train for the last leg of our journey. It was hard to grasp that in a few more hours we would be home. I wasn't sure how I was supposed to feel.

The train was almost full, and because we were the last ones to board we couldn't sit beside each other. I happened to sit beside a man who said his name is Scott. He was sixty-two years old, owned a small farm near West Virginia, and raised goats and hay. He retired from an accounting firm in Pittsburgh and was now a teacher of autistic children and children with emotional problems.

He was a likable man, and he was taking the train to New York to visit a friend. Another nice person to add to our growing list of nice people we probably would never see again on earth. It helped shorten the ride and at 1:45 P.M. we pulled into Lancaster.

Our driver soon showed up to take us home. At 3:00 we pulled into the driveway where I unloaded my baggage, paid the driver, and shouldered the Klutz one more time to carry to the house.

It felt good to be at home, although the humidity took some time to get used to. In the days that followed, I often thought of the Jack Rich quote, "When all is said and done it recharges the part that cannot be seen."

The End